THE
VAULT

THE VAULT

MEMOIRS OF A C-MINUS CHRISTIAN

G. R. GUEST

XULON PRESS

Xulon Press
2301 Lucien Way #415
Maitland, FL 32751
407.339.4217
www.xulonpress.com

© 2022 by G. R. GUEST

All rights reserved solely by the author. The author guarantees all contents are original and do not infringe upon the legal rights of any other person or work. No part of this book may be reproduced in any form without the permission of the author.

Due to the changing nature of the Internet, if there are any web addresses, links, or URLs included in this manuscript, these may have been altered and may no longer be accessible. The views and opinions shared in this book belong solely to the author and do not necessarily reflect those of the publisher. The publisher therefore disclaims responsibility for the views or opinions expressed within the work.

Unless otherwise indicated, Scripture quotations taken from the King James Version (KJV) – *public domain.*

Scripture quotations taken from the English Standard Version (ESV). Copyright © 2001 by Crossway, a publishing ministry of Good News Publishers. Used by permission. All rights reserved.

Paperback ISBN-13: 978-1-66286-721-7
Ebook ISBN-13: 978-1-66286-722-4

DEDICATION

To my lover my wife, my friend and confidant.
Mother, grandmother and great grandmother.
"Her children rise up and call her blessed;
Her husband also, and he praises her saying,
'Many women have done excellently,
but you surpassed them all.'"
Proverbs 31:28-29

Contents

Foreword by Elizabeth Heaney....................ix
Acknowledgments xi
Introduction................................xiii

Chapter 1	Rudy and Chester's Farm 1
Chapter 2	Wonderfully Awful.................. 13
Chapter 3	Red Brick Home................... 17
Chapter 4	Christmas........................ 29
Chapter 5	The Big Move..................... 33
Chapter 6	The Best Grandparents Ever 39
Chapter 7	The Forty-Acre Farm 45
Chapter 8	Hayseed and the Watering Hole. 53
Chapter 9	Adolf Hitler's Meaner Brother......... 57
Chapter 10	Daniel Boone 67
Chapter 11	Spitnella and the T-Bone 83
Chapter 12	The Burlington Northern 91
Chapter 13	A Tiny Town on a Huge Prairie 113

Chapter 14	Northern Canada Evangelical Mission	119
Chapter 15	The Time Machine	129
Chapter 16	Finding Home	155
Chapter 17	"We All Got A Row To Hoe"	171
Chapter 18	Father and Son's Great Adventure	183
Chapter 19	The Bitterroot River	193
Chapter 20	Life on the Big Ditch	201
Chapter 21	Bear Cub Lane	209
Chapter 22	So Many Blessings	215

Foreword

Through George's expressive storytelling, you're invited along on a thoroughly-engaging journey. Looking back across the landscape of his memories, George's distinctive prose often reads like poetry. His stories welcome the reader into a world so vividly described, so beautifully rendered, you'll feel like you're right there when a behemoth train blasts past, overwhelming a tiny boy who's drawn to its raw, ferocious power. His love for the grandparents who offered him emotional refuge embraces you with both the warmth of their embrace and the heartbreak of their loss. As George prays toward the sunrise, you'll feel a certain quietude seep into your heart.

It's rare to witness such a deeply-soulful reckoning of one's life, and George's rich, poignant, funny, animated recollections create a remarkable journey for a reader's heart and spirit.

These stories are simply a wonderful gift, and I hope you'll feel as grateful as I did to have read them.

Elizabeth Heaney, MA, LPC
Author of *The Honor Was Mine: An Insider Look at the Struggles of Military Veterans*

Acknowledgments

Thanks to Jack Retzer, who told me to "start writing things down" about twenty years ago.

Thanks to Vikki Spencer, M.Ed., who found the book hidden in a labyrinth of neurons.

Thanks to Elizabeth Heaney, MA, LPC, who gave me a world of encouragement.

A big thank you to my wife Millie, who did uncounted hours of work on this book.

A special thanks to Maxine Pond, Ed.D., for endless hours of reading, editing, and advising.

OLD WORN MEMORIES

Had a dog named penny, my rifle was a stick,
I was Davy Crockett, just a wandering up the Crick.
The very first boy to ever stepped there,
I killed three Cougars and a grizzly bear.

Picking through Navy beans, looking for a stone
The happiest place was my grandpa's home.
Kids in the bushes, kids in the trees,
Grandma had babies on both her knees.

Spider spinning webs the whole night through,
Strung with diamonds from the morning dew.
Fall colors bright 'neath a buttermilk sky
Down by the Creek where the blackbirds fly.

An old outhouse with quarter-moon door,
Been covered with brambles since '64
A rusty old windmill spinning in the sky,
Squeaking out a memory of days gone by.

"Old worn memories from long ago
I look them all over when I'm feeling low
they're all you have left when you get old.
I wouldn't trade a single one for silver or gold."

Introduction

There is an unseen vault safely hidden in a labyrinth of neurons. That is where I keep some of my most valued possessions. Memories, all kinds of them; some are happy and some are sad. We all make them as we go through the long years of our lives. In my vault there are boxes full of memories on the floor and piled in dusty corners. Some memories are faded and frail, brittle pieces that can no longer tell a tale but still carry in them feelings mysterious and melancholy. It has become quite a mess in there, you know. After all these years I wish I could clean it up a little, but I can't; what's there is there. In Hamlet Act 1 is that all-consuming line, "to thine own self be true." I didn't understand that notion when I was younger, but it is a sore vexation to me now. So many words should have gone unspoken, so many deeds for which I am ashamed, a lot of junk. All that I saw, all that I did, all that I am, it is all in the vault. I try to keep a drop cloth over that pile of junk. I think we'll just leave it alone for now. When I was a small boy, I had no concept of this "vault" that I now speak of. And people don't refer to a vault, they say "oh I remember old so and so."

The Vault

Only when you get older like I am now you find yourself spending more and more time in the vault. Shelves line the walls, and it is here where I keep some of my best memories. Some are funny, even hilarious, happy ones for sure. Others are profound and curious. Some are sweet, sad and lonely. But there is one here I'd like to show you. It is in a worn and tattered old shoe box, carefully tied up in butcher's twine. Written on the end with a purple crayon in a child's handwriting are the words Rudy & Chester's Farm. Let's have a look.

CHAPTER 1
Rudy And Chester's Farm

B ack in the 40's and 50's, automobiles were starting to be considered a necessity. To my grandfather who was born eleven years after the Battle of the Little Big Horn, street cars were the norm; automobiles were the oddity. The generation before that walked or rode a horse, so the forty miles from Minneapolis out to Rudy & Chester's farm was considered a great distance. Back then, there was no such a thing as hopping in a car and taking off. You had to plan ahead for a trip that big, check the oil, kick the tires, and put in a dollar's worth of gas. If the weather was cold, mom would warm bricks in the oven and lay them on the floor boards under our feet. Seems to me we planned these trips out weeks in advance. We loaded the car, packed a lunch, and then we'd be *"off in a cloud of horse feathers."* City streets would slowly give way to open roads and green fields dotted with farm houses. If mom had driven as slow as twenty-five miles an hour all the way, it couldn't have taken two hours to get there, but it seemed like it took forever. That 1936 Ford became a prison for boys, and I was doing hard time, asking every ten minutes "are we almost there??"

But eventually, we would arrive and the sound of their gravel driveway crunching under our tires was like music to my ears. All 4 doors flew open at the same time, and then there ensued the happy hugging's and hellos.

Rudy and my mom had been best of friends in school. My aunt told me "Rudy was tuff as nails," and became their defender as kids. If anybody tried to mess with them, she said Rudy would "punch them out." I didn't know if Rudy was short for Ruth or if it was just a nickname. I do know however that she came from a poor family and was twenty years younger than Chester. Back in the depression days her marriage to Chester was probably arranged.

Now as I recall, along their driveway there was a row of trees to the right, and beyond that a huge corn field. Did you know that if you are only three or four feet tall you can get lost in a corn field? On the left was the old frame house. Beyond that was the implement yard where Chester parked all of the farm equipment in neat rows. He never got rid of a thing. When he replaced say a plow or a harrow or a rake, they all ended up in the rows. Chester was encouraged to sell off the old scrap metal for the war effort but he wouldn't do it. He would use parts off the old equipment to fix the new. Straight ahead was the biggest building on the farm, the cow barn. Between the house and the barn was the outhouse and corn crib. I think the spring house was attached to the barn.

Every nook and cranny on that dairy holds a happy memory for me, even the outhouse! It was so different, fun to use, and you never got hollered at for forgetting to flush. The Sears & Roebuck's Catalog was within easy reach, as it was in all outhouses of the time. What a wonderful service they rendered, free of charge! They gave you all kinds of pictures to look at, while you waited for nature to run its course, and they improved the personal hygiene of rural America. Because of that outhouse, I know why the glossy pages were the last ones to leave the catalog! You can't buy that kind of knowledge. You'll never find it in any university, and it's sad to say, those of us who know are a dying breed. Outhouses were a peaceful place of thoughtful contemplation. I wish we could bring them back. Many years later I was telling this story to a group of seniors and when I got to the glossy page part an eighty-year-old woman popped right up and said that they used to take those glossy pages and rub them between their hands to make them more absorbent. I guess we keep learning new stuff every day.

Next to the outhouse was the corn crib. This was another curious object you never saw in the city. If I close my eyes, I can see myself a small boy, walking slowly around the corn crib, carefully examining each side. It had a more or less normal roof, but the sides were horizontal slats about two inches apart, so the corn could dry. The longer sides were narrow at the bottom and flared out at the top. Inside, it was filled to the top with long, yellow ears of dried corn. It was wonderful to look at because it and everything else on this farm was so different from life in the city; I was so attracted to it. I loved my mom, but I was sure the stork had made a mistake and dropped me off at the wrong house. Here was where I belonged. I remember sunny patches in the yard, the wonderful cow smell in the barn, and the muted clapping of their bells. Some kids would have considered the corn crib a great thing to climb on, but not me. I was happy just to study it, ponder how well it fit in, and thankful it was there.

The barn was the grandest of all, towering high over all the farm. It was the business end of the dairy. It was the biggest building I had ever been in. The cavernous hay loft was so huge it made you feel no bigger than a mouse. We were there one time when they were putting up hay in the barn. I have bucked a lot of bales in my life, but this was the one and only time I ever saw hay put up loose. Work went on there morning and evening, in sickness and in health, in fair weather or foul. When city folks sat by the fire on Christmas Eve drinking hot chocolate and eggnog, Rudy and Chester were milking cows. When factory workers were sleeping off a New Year's hangover, Rudy and Chester were milking cows. When families gathered on the Fourth of July, eating apple pie and ice cream and waiting for the fireworks, Rudy and Chester were milking cows. It was obvious that they took pride in what they had and did because the whole farm was kept neat as a pin, including the barn. But their fondness for that barn could never exceed the joy and happiness we found there. What amounted to 365 days of work to them was all fun and games to us kids.

When milking time rolled around, everybody knew exactly what to do, including the cows. When the cow door was opened, they would parade into the milking parlor like obedient children returning to class. Each one would go to their appropriate place, and just like children there was always a dummy or two who would poke their heads into the wrong stanchion and have to be reminded of their proper place. Somehow Rudy & Chester seemed to know one cow from the other. They were all black and white, and looked exactly alike to me. I don't recall if they had names for them, but they knew each one and what to expect from them. When the cows were in their stanchions they formed 2 long rows, heads all facing the center of the barn. There was a narrow walkway between their heads where Chester could feed the cows and lock them into their stanchions. Chester was very calm and nonchalant about the walkway, like there was nothing to it. I was scared to death of that walkway full of cows with their long tongues licking up the hay, but I had to do it. Chester needed my help. I remember having both arms wrapped tightly around Chester's leg, holding on for dear life, hiding my face in his baggy overalls. The cows became quite curious about this new attachment on Chester. As we passed awkwardly on, each cow would stretch out their necks so they could sniff, snort, and blow snot in my face. I didn't mind the snot as long as they didn't eat me! For many years, that bovine gauntlet became the mental picture that appeared when someone would read Psalm 23; the part about "yea though I walk through the valley of the shadow of death," but I would not be afraid, because Chester was with me!

I don't think I spent much time in the house. I have no clear picture of its layout. I do remember the heavenly smell of home-made bread and the best of home cooking. There was a thin wire stretched across the kitchen window over the sink. That is where Chester hung his tea bag that he would use for the whole week. It was a daily ritual to watch Chester drink his tea and eat his cake. As many times as we visited their home, it was always done exactly the same way. We all carefully watched. He would pour a cup of hot water, unclip the tea bag from the wire over the sink, give it a quick dunk in his cup, then reattach it to the wire with a clothes pin, ready for the next day's use. He would sit at the table, sip the tea, and eat the large square of white cake in two huge bites. I don't know how many times we have commented on this oddity of his down through the years, but he never let us down. Chester was a creature of habit. He seemed a kind, quiet man, and had lots of patience with us kids. He would let my brother drive the Farmall tractor all by himself. It is funny the things your mind holds onto. I remember clear as a bell my brother exclaiming after driving the tractor that it could "turn on a dime." His excitement was real enough, but the literal interpretation made no sense. My mind tried to conjure up an ant-sized tractor running around in circles on a dime. I filed it away with all of the other mysteries of life. I was too small to solo, so Chester set me on his lap and we'd drive all over the farm, my hands on the steering wheel, sure

I was the one driving. I remember a place that was always wet and muddy. Chester went right through the middle of it. The thick mud squished up between the front tires. How wonderful was that! In the country, even grown-ups got to play in the mud. Oh, how I loved this place!

One day, I unintentionally locked Chester in the barn. I had latched the hook on the outside of the barn door, not knowing Chester was inside. I never got scolded for it because Rudy thought it was hilarious. But it created quite a problem for poor old Chester because it was the only way in and out of the barn, except of course where the cows came in. I think that is what tickled Rudy and sent her into fits of knee-slapping laughter. It was a large door on rollers that opened sideways on the far end of the barn. Outside that door was a sea of mud, churned up twice daily by eighteen cows coming in and out of the milking parlor. This was the most disagreeable option, but it was clear nobody heard his banging and hollering. He could stay in the barn all day, or go out the cow door. Neither of them had ever gone out this way before; there was no reason to until I came along. He slid the door open far enough to squeeze through and stood on the concrete apron looking dubiously at the soupy landscape. It was fifteen to twenty feet in either direction to dry ground. I suppose he thought that if he stayed close to the barn, he might be okay. But it was no good. When he slid off the edge of the concrete, it was too deep. The "moo-poo" soup flowed over the top of his boots. It was a nasty piece of work getting out of the barn that way, but he never said a word about it, at least not to me. I would have been devastated if I thought Chester was mad at me.

Rudy was a slender, healthy, attractive young woman. She was fun loving, and a smile came easy and often to her face. The hard life on the farm had made her as strong as any man. She would hold her arms out to the side and let us kids swing on them like they were tree branches. When milking was done and dinner happily eaten, Rudy would get her guitar out and we would sing and laugh and talk into the starry night. I was too young to understand such things then, but when I look back at her now, I would have to say Rudy was probably one of those people who was just full of mischief. I remember her changing the words to the song "My Bonnie Lies Over the Ocean" to "My Fanny Lies Over the Nail Keg." Rudy was much younger than Chester. They never had children of their own. Some say it was the hard years of the great depression that brought this young girl from a poor family into Chester's life. I wonder now if they found happiness in each other. I hope so, because I found it in them. Rudy and Chester were undoubtedly flawed with faults and foibles common to us all, but not to me. I see them through the eyes of a child. They were the caretakers of Heaven, and I found no fault in them. I loved them with a Godly sort of love, often found in the child but lost in the adult. That is where they have been for all these years, and that is where they will stay;

In a worn and tattered old shoe box carefully tied up in butcher's twine.

Chester and I

My brother and sister with Rudy

In December of 1987 I didn't have enough money to buy my brother and sister anything for Christmas so I wrote the following song for them;

RUDY AND CHESTER

We were living in the city then' but mama she had a friend
Who owned a farm not forty miles away.
We'd start out early in the day in a '37 Chevrolet,
And we'd drive all day to get to Rudy's farm.
They had a million cows all black and white
With great big horns to scare a tike,

Rudy And Chester's Farm

And a hayloft like a big 'ol feather bed,
Where all us kids could laugh and play
Chasin' chickens all the day
And an old frame house that smelled of homemade bread.

Chorus: And I want to go back, back to younger days.
Back where your dreams come true.
And I want to go back, back to childhood ways,
At times it seems the best that we can do.

Milking cows and loading hay, chopping wood for colder days,
And us kids would want to help with everything;
After supper that house would ring,
When Rudy'd play her ole six string
And the rest of us would clap our hands and sing.
Sears and roebucks wishing book in the outhouse had its nook,
And an old spring house that kept the creamery cold;
I think that farmer liked me the best
In spite of my mischievousness,
Cause Chester had no son when he was old.
Chorus:

CHAPTER 2
WONDERFULLY AWFUL

When I'm in the vault I'm still a small child. With my eyes closed I can see myself putting Rudy and Chester back in its place on the top shelf, I have to stand on my tippy toes to reach. I look around in wonder at all the stories; I know I've seen them all, but I am a child and I don't remember in the moment making all that this room contains. Poking around in a box on the floor I see a lot of stuff about trains.

We lived only two blocks from the railroad tracks that ran behind the big Purina feed mill on Hiawatha Avenue in Minneapolis. Back in the 50s steam locomotives were still in use and I remember well my first close encounter with one of the really big mainline locomotives. I was pretty young, maybe four or five years old. Mother and I were going somewhere in our '36 Ford when we came to a railroad crossing. As we approached the crossing the lights came on, a bell started to ring, and the gate dropped down right in front of our car. This had never happened before, being right next to the gate, and I knew what it meant; a train was coming.

I looked out to my right, and sure enough there was a huge steam locomotive coming for all it was worth. A tremendous volume of pitch-black smoke was boiling profusely out of the stack, leaving the whole length of the train swaddled in a wondrous black cloud. This was going to be positively wonderful. Then I thought of something that would make it even better. I turned to mom and asked her if we could get out of the car and stand right next to the crossing gate so I could get the best possible view. To my surprise she said "Okay."

So, with my little hand held tightly in hers, we stepped up to the crossing. The train was already closer, bigger, it's approaching speed more obvious. The clang, clang, clang from the crossing signal occupied every square inch of space with an overpowering sense of urgency, and I am quite sure the steam powered whistle could be heard by a deaf man. I could feel the vibration inside the marrow of my bones, and it turned my mind to red. Closer now, I could see the push rods going back and forth driving the huge steel wheels. It seemed an impossibility that anything so big could move so fast. It reminded me of watching mom run her sewing machine; the needle ran up and down so fast it would almost disappear. This was like that but only much bigger. Between the whistle blasts, I could hear the rapid "Chu, Chu, Chu" sound and see little bits of steam hissing out here and there. It was all so busy, so huge; it was alive, huffing and puffing, steaming, clanging bell and screaming whistle, so explosively intent on its labor, driven by hell's own fire. It cared only for pulling and pulling. It seemed impossible that such a tremendous beast could be controlled by a mere man. This was all getting to be more than I expected. My eager desire to have the closest possible view was completely satisfied. I had gone through joy to happiness, excitement escalated up to awesome, topping out at thrilling. When the ground started to shake, I was aware of new emotions. But there was no time to put a name to it, because the beautiful, wonderful, awful thing was upon us. Its approaching wind hit and left us all awash in the dragon's steamy, oily smelling breath. As it thundered through the crossing, I looked up and there, dream-like through the haze, I saw the engineer leaning out of the window and giving me a huge wave. I caught his knowing smile, just before my mind was completely toasted.

This event became something omnipotent to me, and blistered the paint off of my mental picture of trains. The trains I had imagined were not so huge and powerful. My trains were friendly, something you could control. When I stood at the crossing in the presence of the real thing, I was devastated. In less time than it takes to wind a clock, I experienced something that was so wonderful it was awful. I did the only thing a little boy could do; I wet my pants and started to cry.

This story reminds me of yet another crossing. We're all coming to it. Whether I want to think about it or not, I will someday soon stand in the presence of the one who spoke the universe into existence. I wonder will it be like this?

Will God be bigger and more powerful than I expected? Will He be "wonderfully Awful?" I do have this tendency to create God in my own image just as I had done with the train, ignore what is written in scripture and give God small thoughts, reassuring words and man-centered motives. I know some people try to do away with God altogether, saying there is no God. But the Bible tells us "His invisible attributes are clearly seen" in his creation. He has written his law in our hearts and our consciences. "We are without excuse." To say you don't believe in God makes about as much sense as saying you don't believe in trains. But when you're in the middle of the crossing, the existence of the train is not dependent on your belief in it, your awareness of it, or your false image of it. Like God, the train is. The good news is that the road on the other side of the crossing goes ever on and on, if you can make it across, that is. God, through his Son, has made for us a safe crossing. It's the only way. Jesus said "I am the way, the truth, and the life; no man comes to the Father but through me." (John 14:6

CHAPTER 3
RED BRICK HOME

In the vault, on the second shelf, far to the right sat a thin, flat manila folder. There was my name, last name first, my case number and the name of the welfare worker, Mrs. Boo. I walked over to it and laid my small hand on it. Profound sadness, confusion and sorrow came into my mind. I don't open this one very often any more. I use to keep it open all the time because it was evidence against a small boy who really didn't know why this happened.

The way I felt about myself in the following pages really began when I was only four or five. My mother had gone out on a date, and returning home late she found she had forgot her house keys. She banged and banged on the door trying to wake one of her three children in the upstairs bedrooms. I remember getting up and going down the stairs to a landing halfway down where there was a small window. I saw two people walking away from the house and thought in my half-awake mind that whoever it was they didn't want to come in, so I went back to bed. I loved my mother so much. I was a mama's boy. The next morning when I found out what I had done, I was horrified. I had locked my mother outside all night in the cold. I wouldn't even let her in the house. In my mind I saw her walking the dark streets wondering why her little boy wouldn't let her in the house. I didn't say a word to anyone. But I started hating myself for what I had done. I cried unseen and unheard for years and years over this awful thing. Decades of low self-esteem started right here. I began gathering regrets along the way, like a beach comber picking up driftwood. I opened the folder, slipped out the pages, and started to read:

It was early summer of 1956 and as mom used to say; *"the snow is gone, the grass is riz, I wonder where the birdies is."* The possibilities for an eight-year-old boy on such a beautiful day should have been endless. But slowly I became aware of some problems which involved me in a life changing way. First, I was told I had failed the third grade; well, I thought that's ok, its summertime, who cares about school now. Right! Then they told me I had something called; dyslexia. Well here again, I couldn't even pronounce it so what's the big deal. Well, it was about to become a big deal because on that very day I became the youngest resident of a Minnesota state run orphanage. Don't ask me why. Ok, so you think you have to know why so I'll tell you this much. I think it started on a day Dad came for a visit and found me in a ratty, worn-out pair of shoes. I could be wrong about this, but shoes were a big deal to my dad. He grew up in the great depression and had to put cardboard in his shoes to cover the holes, and no kid of his was going to run around in ratty shoes. He never missed a child support check, not one. So where was the money going? My dad had friends in high places and he got the welfare department involved, and that's all I'm going to say. As a parent I've made horrible mistakes I wish I could undo, and I hope my kids will have the charity to overlook some of them. Besides it doesn't matter anymore. With my clothes and a few toys in the back of the car we were off to the orphanage.

It was of the old institutional style orphanage, unlike today's group homes. The staff worked hourly shifts, and I don't remember becoming attached to any save for the cook. The building was large and foreboding, it looked like a prison. In fact, it was, for children. It was built of red brick, three stories tall with all the homines of a tire factory. The top floor was for the girls, the second for the boys and the main floor had a big common space. The first floor also had a cafeteria style dining room and a large commercial kitchen with a locking door. Once I learned the pecking order, that lock and the cook became very important to me.

I can remember three people clearly, the aforementioned cook, a girl about fifteen or sixteen years old, and the bully. Oh yes, there was this counselor who had me by a leg and one arm swinging me around and around doing the air plane thing. That was fun, sort of, until he lost his balance and ran me head first into a five-inch water main that ran up the wall. I suppose the going wage for that sort of job did not attract the best and the brightest. I was out cold for five minutes, and when I came to, the cook, the girl and the bully, plus everyone in the orphanage were gathered round to see if the kid was going to make it.

There is a lot more discussion today on the subject of bullying, but not then. You were on your own. There was this one little turd, I don't remember his name, but his only function in life was to bedevil my every waking moment. He would hit me, push me down, trip me, take my toys, and worst of all he would do his best to humiliate me. I remember one time he held a club over my head and told me he would hit me with it if I didn't take down my pants. It would make a good story now if I could tell you how I finally got even with the little turd, but I didn't. The lock on the kitchen door became my only defense. I was always faster than most kids, so if I made it through the kitchen door in time and set the lock, I would be safe for a while. Most children learn by this age to fight back, to defend against bullies, to ask for help. But mistreatment and cruelty I reasoned was my do. I had failed third grade, I had this dyslexia thing, and now I was in this orphanage. Plus, from the earliest age I had learned to hate myself; I don't know why. Maybe the devil made me do it. But somehow, I had it coming, so it was all right. (I must interject here that this is poor theology. The devil cannot make us do anything, but he can sure lie to us.)

Looking back at my time of incarceration, I realize it was the girl who had by far the biggest effect on me. So much of her is missing now; she was older than me by four or five years. I don't remember her name or what she looked like, but she colored my life with a wonderful, dreamy, lonesome kind of mystery. She had a really good voice and loved to sing, and it was her who introduced me to the great art of yodeling. I remember like it was yesterday, telling my mother over the telephone about this girl who could yodel and how I thought it was the most beautiful thing I had ever heard. As it turns out my mother knew a lot about it, and though she could not yodel herself, she was able to teach me the basics over the phone. I have been a happy yodeler all my life. I would listen to her singing along with the radio. There was this one song in particular that I still remember the tune and a handful of words. I have never been able to find it anywhere and haven't heard it since. As often as I would sing the part I remembered, memories of her always filled me with a sad, happy feeling, as if part of her still inhabited the melody. I guess being only eight or nine years old she would qualify as my first love. I didn't understand such things then, infatuation was still years beyond me. But I would do anything, including stealing cigarettes for her. Now if that isn't love, what is?

I became very ill that summer, rheumatic fever, I think. They moved me to the third floor, I guess so the girls could help care for me. After bed time there was probably only a night watchman around, so it was up to the girls to look after me. This is where the word mystery presents itself in my story. Of what happened up there I have no recollection, but I know something changed in me as a result of it. Something I can't put a value to, no sense of good or bad, right or wrong, it is like finding myself in a strange room hung everywhere with dusty gossamer vails blocking my view of the room. I try to see what happened in there, but I can't. It was very puzzling as a child; I was left with a feeling I could not put a name to, as if some kind- of magic were involved. Today I can imagine what power could have generated this feeling, this mystery. Was it the girl? I think so. Was it a violation? If it was, after all these years I have no stones to throw at her. Only it did have a real lasting effect. It's like an old steel drum rusting away in some dump, what comes leaking out the bottom are just two words; too soon.

As I had stated earlier, I was given the opportunity to redo the third grade, you know, stay back and be a leader in the next school year. I don't recall if I felt like a leader or not, but I do remember getting some tips on spelling one word in particular. And with encouragement from some of the older boys, and a piece of chalk, I wrote that word in two-foot-high block letters on the front of the orphanage; F_ _ K! I didn't know what it meant, and I didn't learn that day either, except it was something really bad. I spent two hours washing it off with a brush and a bucket of water. I'm sure I must have been a favorite among the staff.

I remember a dream I had at the orphanage. Standing on the curb out front, I would hold my arms out just like Peter Pan. Then jumping off the curb I would fly across the road almost touching the pavement and then I would catch the air, swoop up and land perfectly on the opposite curb. I did it over and over again, it was so much fun. That became the high-water mark of flying dreams for me. It was so real I had to try it the next day, but all I got for the effort was a good hard landing on the pavement.

This orphanage was another piece of evidence that proved beyond doubt that I was some kind of world class loser. In this case, there was one difference. It was not a mistake I made. This is not one of things I keep under the drop cloth on the vault floor. I was a simple case of collateral damage between two warring factions - my divorced parents. At the end of that summer, after school started, I was moved to my dad's home. He was unable to give his new wife children, and I was the youngest of his three. Maybe I was her pick. They would have been better off had they gone after my sister; she loved her dad with an unerring love. But I didn't know him; I have no memory of him living in our house. And whenever he did come around, he was angry. My father won that battle but lost the war, to which I give him my highest admiration. I loved my mother, and in the end, he came to understand that. I went to spend Christmas with mom and never returned. When my dad died at the age of fifty-eight, the first thought that came into my mind was, I had never told him that I loved him. Oh my, another regret, just what I needed.

People say; "winners never quit, and losers never win." But I say if you never win and you never quit, you're stupid. For almost half of my younger life, I was being carefully groomed for my own destruction. I took my negative self-image, which I involved myself in the making, and I wrapped it like a filthy rag around my heart and hoped to find some perverse comfort in it. I made an exercise of magnifying my failures and sabotaging my successes. Worse than that, low self-esteem becomes a safety net for the under achiever. It gives you an excuse to never try; I couldn't do it, I'm not good enough, I'm not smart enough, etc. It makes you lazy, it stifles your potential, and it keeps you on the bench while others play the game. This is a common condition among young people, but more than that, I believe it is by satanic design. I have to ask who benefits when a four-year-old boy learns to loathe himself? It makes no sense unless you factor evil into the equation. "Be sober and vigilant; because your adversary the devil walks about like a roaring lion, seeking whom he may devour." 1 Peter 5:8. Satan's only goal is to destroy all he can of God's creation. But here's the rub; he has to get our permission to do it. How do we give him permission? By believing his dirty little lies. There was a saying that popped up in the late 70s "God don't make no junk." Poor grammar, but it's true. If you believe God is your redeemer, then you must believe He is also your creator, because He made you and loves you just the way you are. No one could change the way I thought about myself, **only I could**. The same is true for anyone who wants to be free of it.

My mother was artistic in so many ways. She wrote songs and poems. She loved music, nature, and the God of nature. She made life fun – and – she was chronically impractical. My father was very intelligent, a man of integrity, faithful, and although it didn't always show on the outside, he was kind. He was all business. Things were either black or white, and he could spot B.S. a mile away, like the time I suggested that

I was stupid. His response was a quick kick in the butt! He was pragmatic and practical. My mother was the dreamer. My father was the Gestapo (I mean this in the kindest possible way). They were both very good-looking people, which I'm sure is what drew them together in the first place, like Scarlet O'Hara and Rhett Butler. Wow! What a gorgeous couple!

But they never should have been allowed to have children! The physical love that overlooks a multitude of sins in the beginning could not maintain in the long haul a dreamer and a Gestapo. The inevitable explosion came twelve years later, she left with 3 kids and a house, and he left with a growing pile of canceled child support checks.

But my brother, sister, and I came away with a little DNA from them both, each of us containing varying amounts of matter and antimatter. For myself, I wanted to be a dreamer but I came away with equal amounts of them both, so the war that began between them continued on inside of me. O to be carefree, to enjoy life to follow your dreams! I need to get a job, I have bills to pay and children to raise, I must become practical. When I allowed the dreamer more room to wander around in my mind and surface now and then, I was as happy and creative as I have ever been in my life. But then the ass kicker would show up and demand I plow under that meadow full of wild flowers I was growing and plant a cash crop, whatever would pay the most. I wanted babbling brook, moss and fern, but I ended up with steel, smoke, and concrete.

My kids will probably write someday about the man who raised them, when they have time to ponder how I did. Sorry, I say to them, sorry for the fight that consumed so much of all I was, or could have been or done.

The Gestapo is old now and tired, and the dreamer has become practical. I forgive them both. I have to, because I love them, mom, dad, the dreamer, the Gestapo. They, being forever at odds, need each other like a battery needs a positive and a negative to do what it needs to do. The dreamer overlooks and forgives others, loves to sing and play, very industrious at having fun, tirelessly hopeful. But it "wants what it wants, or else it does not care," (Emily Dickinson), regardless of what is right or wrong. The dreamer is a sinner!

So, you see I needed the Gestapo; he gets things done. Being practical is a real drag, but even the dreamer has to admit that we would have run our financial ship aground many times if he had the tiller. Knowing that what I'm thinking is truth or B.S. is called wisdom, something that's in short supply these days. So, my advice to you is, as much as possible, live at peace with yourself and with God, and don't take life too seriously. In the end, the Bible says our many years are "but a vapor."

I just hope my little "vapor" had a pleasant odor.

I didn't know it but our time in Minneapolis was coming to an end. Unbeknownst to my father or us kids, mom had sold our house and had all our stuff shipped out to Vancouver Washington. She was afraid my dad would try to stop her from moving his kids out of state. Well, she pulled that maneuver off with perfection; my dad came for a visit one day and found another family living in the house.

Still in my vault I don't want to leave Minnesota without showing you two things; the first one a picture entitled "The Happy Little Family That Never Was," and secondly a story that goes with it.

Happy Little Family That Never Was

This picture is a singularity – the only one in existence, I being the smallest. I have no memories in the vault of my father living in the house.

CHAPTER 4
Christmas

I can remember so clearly, as if it were yesterday, lying in bed on Christmas eve, listening for any tell-tail sound of reindeer coming from the roof, and trying to imagine how wonderful it must be to have sugar plums dance in your head. Although I really had no idea what a "sugar plum" was, I thought it must be something very sweet that danced around, throwing fairy dust all over in your dreams. I sure wanted some of that!

Christmas was, for me, an enchanting, wonderful mix of images, of houses festooned in colored lights and new-fallen snow, of a brilliant star, a silent night, and a Holy Child in a manger. There was, of course, Santa Claus and his famous flying reindeer, who delivered toys and candy. But then you got stuff from other people like relatives and friends. So, I figured that Santa was there just to prime the pump and get people moving in the right direction. This was a good thing. I identified with Rudolph. He was different, he didn't fit in, and was ostracized by his contemporaries. Like Rudolph, I was hoping that I would someday display an invaluable hidden gift. Christmas morning was the present-opening grand finale, and the conclusion of this holiday. There was an after-glow that lingered for a few days, but for me, the best part was the magic of Christmas Eve. Seeing the "Miracle on 34th Street," the music, the hope, the wonder, the holiness. It was a supernatural event of flying reindeer and talking snowmen. It was those sugar plums.

Around Christmas time, Walt Disney always showed that cartoon of the two chipmunks, Chip & Dale in the Christmas tree. It is a classic you must have seen, with Pluto in hot pursuit as Chip & Dale ran through the branches with nuts and candy canes. I would lie under the tree for hours, mesmerized by the glory of lights, tinsel, and the scent of evergreen. How wonderful, I thought, to be able to scamper up and down the tree and out to the end of the branches. That's where Santa always put candy canes and chocolate on Christmas Eve. Think how huge a candy cane would be if you were the size of a chipmunk! I don't know how many times I must have fallen asleep there, my mind swaddled in such a tapestry of wonder. Maybe this is what Clement Clark Moore had in mind when he wrote about sugar plums dancing in your head.

It all made sense then, but not now. I'm sure I must be related to that boy, that little believer. But I can no longer get the connection between a holy child in the manger and this fat man in a red suit sneaking around into all our houses. It's not a matter of being gullible. That presumes a person should "know better" than to believe in such a story.

No, this is something that predates gullibility. Innocence; the ability to completely and totally believe what you've been told, because an innocent mind is incapable of the very concept of falsehood, especially coming from your mommy. Mother was a gifted story teller. With wide-eyed wonder, I believed every word she said. Mom said that Reindeer could fly, so that was all there was to it. They could fly, and so could Peter Pan. I used to dream I could fly too. Then one day I got this notion that if I started out small, I might be able to do it for real. We had this big ottoman in our living room. I thought I could fly over that for starters, and then move on to something bigger. I stood there with my arms out to the side in classic Peter Pan fashion, concentrated on the ottoman, ran, jumped, and sailed over the ottoman in perfect Peter Pan form. I completely cleared the ottoman, landing flat on the carpet like a World War II bomber, coming down with disabled landing gear. It hurt. But mother was so taken with my little maneuver that I didn't have the heart to tell her. She had me do it over and over when friends or neighbors stopped by. I wish I could hurt that way again.

We were the first ones on our block to have a color TV set, and even back in the days of "Leave It to Beaver" mom had the sense to know that too much television would be bad for us. So, every week our TV "went on the fritz," and just as mysteriously, it would start working again on Saturday night just in time for "Zorro," "Have Gun Will Travel," and best of all "Disney's Wonderful World of Color."

I never caught on, that it was mom pulling the tubes out of the back of the TV.

Santa Claus and sugarplums faded away over the years, as they do in all of us, all that is except for my oldest daughter. Somehow, she has managed to hang on to a few sugar plums. So now, I have become a watcher of grandchildren, and great grandchildren, hoping to see the joy in their faces as they light up with wonder, and if you are looking at just the right instant, you'll see it; that twinkle in their eyes.

That's the fairy dust!

CHAPTER 5
THE BIG MOVE

According to Google Maps it is 1735 miles from Minneapolis, MN to Vancouver, WA. The US Federal Highway Act was signed into law by Dwight D. Eisenhower; it was called the "National Interstate and Defense Highways Act" of June 1956. In 1958 when we made the trip, it was closer to 2000 miles. The roads we drove on back then would be considered secondary roads today and were mostly for getting you from one town to the next, whereas the Interstate was designed to get you from one end of the country to the other. I can't find much in the vault about the trip, maybe I slept most of the way. There is a fragment of paper with the words "I can still see the little white paper bag" on it. Mom must have stopped at a confectionery along the way and purchased some chocolates, the round ones about the size of a quarter covered with little white beads. After we gobbled them up, someone rolled down a window and threw the empty bag out on the road, a common practice in those days. Then one of us kids started something that would last for years. Out of shear boredom one of us said, "I can still see the white paper bag." Then in turn each of us would declare they could see the white paper bag until it was long gone. We kept the game going until mom informed us that we were telling lies, since we could not actually see the white paper bag. So, we changed it to "I can still remember the little white paper bag," something we siblings invoked for years to come. Dumb, but that's kids for you.

My grandfather had taken the train from Vancouver to Minneapolis so he could help my mom with the driving. But grandpa was not that great of a driver; I think his eyes were failing. With some of the proceeds from the sale of the house, mom had purchased a brand new 1958 Pontiac station wagon, and a second-hand camper trailer that we pulled behind the car. One time when grandpa was driving, he passed a lumber truck and must have forgot he was pulling the trailer. He tried to pull back into the right lane too soon, and ended up dragging the trailer down the side of the truck he was passing. He tore a big hole in the side of the trailer.

Lewis and Clark were told by the plains Indians that they would come to the shining mountains as they traveled further West. Traveling at speed 153 years later, we found the very same shining mountains still laden with winter snow. But then something strange seemed to happen, the mountains never got any closer. We drove and drove, but they were still on the horizon the same as before. We were looking at the continental divide for the whole day before it started to present itself visibly closer. Sitting on the vault floor trying to make sense of this faded fragment of a memory, a notion started to form in my mind of why it took so long to get to the mountains. I was raised in Minnesota flatland. If you saw something on the horizon that looked a long way off, it would only be about twelve miles away. The same thing is true if you are standing in the wet sand at the ocean; the curvature of the earth hides anything beyond twelve miles. But the northern Rockies stand at 10,000 feet, so if you are driving over a higher piece of land in the east you could see the mountains from hundreds of miles away.

Continuing on our way to Vancouver, WA, we would have traveled on the Washington side of the Columbia River. I-84 on the Oregon side was not built until 1966. We would have passed right by Celilo Falls, where the indigenous people had fished for over 10,000 years. One year earlier on March 10, 1957, they closed the floodgates on the newly finished Dalles Dam. The local news reported that over 10,000 people lined the hills along the river to watch Celilo Falls become Celilo Lake. It only took four hours to fill the dam.

I don't know how my brother felt about the move, but my sister was devastated at having to leave her father so far behind. As far as I was concerned, it was one big adventure. Life is like that when you're only ten years old. Arriving at the grand old house my grandpa built, opened a whole new chapter for us all. I think it was a good move.

GRANDMA'S HOUSE

In a grand old house, my grandpa-built Generations would assemble
Children running everywhere, In the woods us boys would ramble.
In these happy days of sunshine, we thought we were immortal,
It wasn't time for us to know that there's an end someday.

There's a heavy, oaken rocker that an uncle used to live in,
He never had a lot to say and I'd watch his hands a shaking.
Now the Spirit knows the time when the soul should be taken,
Now there's an empty rocker sitting silent by the wall.

Grandma was the fabric that held us all together
Summer days were long then, I thought life would last forever.
Then one Sunday morning, Gabriel stretched his hands down from heaven,
Turned another page of life, now grandma does not live here anymore.

It's a sad and lonely feeling when you think of life this way,
We're the old ones caring for the younger, we must lead the way.
We must bear the burden, we're the ones who know life's sorrows,
Dreaming of our yesterdays,
They're hopeful for the joys of life's tomorrows.

Chorus:
It's the young ones getting older, and the old ones pass away;
It's just another fact of life
From which mankind is not allowed to stray.

So, hold your loved ones in your hearts today.

CHAPTER 6
THE BEST GRANDPARENTS EVER

I could go on and on here telling you about our grandparents. They were the quintessential couple, and over the next ten years of my life they created an unchanging, stable and happy environment. Grandpa was an artist by trade, but he could do just about anything with wood. Besides the aforementioned grand old house, he built a sixteen-foot sailboat that we all sailed in. He made his own bow and arrows; he was a good gunsmith and kept bees for their honey. He was a quiet, honorable man who loved reading Zane Grey and Louis L'Amour books. With a house full of noisy grandkids, he would turn his hearing aid down and be lost in his reading. We would often hear him chuckling to himself about something he found humorous in the story.

Grandma, truly was "the fabric that held us all together." She occupied at least four stations in life. Number one, she was always squeezing one of her beloved grandchildren into her pillowy bosom. Number two, in the kitchen cooking. I remember her at the kitchen counter one time stirring with some effort a huge bowl of pancake batter. Her full-size waist would start to gyrate in rhythm with the spoon. Number three, Grandma kept a big vegetable garden and lots of flowers. But I think her forth and favorite thing by far was her chickens. When out in the back yard, she didn't just care for them, she communed with them. With her apron full of grain, her hens would gather around her like eager students around a beloved schoolmarm. She would cluck to them, throwing out handfuls of feed. It was magical! They had absolutely no fear of her because my grandma was a chicken charmer.

Seeing her with them so long ago put a spell on me, and I have loved chickens ever since. As a matter of fact, it's been reported that on an earlier visit to grandma's house at the age of four, I presented myself at the big house with a chicken under each arm, both dead, throttled. Evidently, I hadn't mastered the "charming" part yet.

But I studied chickens, and as you will see, there's a lot you can say about them. They will wake you up in the morning, and provide eggs for breakfast, cold-cuts for lunch, and chicken & dumplings for dinner. They will let you know when they've laid an egg, and then go on endlessly clucking and buck- bucking like there was nothing else to talk about. I still love to watch how they work the ground. We've all seen them do this; they take a step forward, and go scratch-scratch with the left foot, scratch-scratch with the right, then stepping back they cock their heads and carefully examine their diggings like a prospector looking for gold, all the while making contented little sounds that blend into warm afternoons, a feeling of peace.

Now don't let my grandchildren hear this, but they are marvelously fun to chase! Though your stature in the human world may be small and meek, a chicken can always be depended upon to run when chased because, well, because they are chickens, and they are great at the game. They don't run straight away, but bob and weave, and run around buildings and trees; you really have to focus.

There were two exceptions to the game of chase and run. A hen with chicks, even though obviously disturbed by your presence, would stand her ground. With wings unfurled, she would face off with you while chicks scurried around her like electrons around an atom.

Then there was Roscoe the rooster, the infamous backyard bully. Grandma was too busy to be on hand to scold us every time we took to chasing her beloved hens, so she employed Roscoe to do the job. The only thing bigger than his spurs was his ego. He was meaner than a junk-yard dog. A master of surprise and attack, he would circle around and come in from the side or back and go to work on you with wings and spurs. He would put the whole chase in reverse; now I would be the chicken, running pell-mell out of the back yard. It added that wonderful element of danger. I don't know if he took time off to eat or sleep. He was always on guard, watching for one of us to cross the line onto his turf.

The Vault

Life always provides you with a bully or two, in your neighborhood, on the playground, in the office, or at the job site, and if you allow them the opportunity, they can be a real pain. One day, I formed a plan to deal with Roscoe once and for all. I found a piece of lath, and I held it behind my back so he couldn't see it. Then I walked right past the chicken house, and sure enough, there he was. When he spotted me, I could see feathers around his neck start to rise in preparation for his attack. I turned and pretended to run as usual, but when I figured he had time to come into range, I turned and swung the lath like a baseball bat. I caught Roscoe right on the back of the head and killed him.

What?! Wait, I didn't want to do that, just scare him a little! But there he was, lying there lifeless on the ground. I had just killed Grandma's rooster! I looked up, and there were 100 eyes from all the hens staring at me and at what I had done. They stood still, comprehension coming slowly that the boy, who from time to time had been only a nuisance, had now become a murderer! I had to do something fast. Any moment now, someone could come around the back and see guilty Cain standing over innocent Able. I remembered what the preacher said about Cain and what God was going to do to him, and like Cain, I had a corpse to hide. I pulled poor "Able" over to the chicken house and used the piece of lath to push him underneath. I hoped that when he was found, that suspicion would not fall on me.

I disposed of the murder weapon and ran for the raspberry patch, where I spent the next two hours living the life of a fugitive. Oh, how black the day had become. I knew the call for supper was not far away, and I was tired of running, tired of the guilt. I was going to turn myself in. The path back to grandma's house, and to judgment, led by the chicken yard. As I passed by, I looked over at the chicken yard, expecting to see the accusing hens lined up like a gauntlet, eager to see justice done to this guilty boy. But everything looked just like it always looked; the chickens were here and there, pecking and scratching the ground, and they hardly took notice of my passing.

Then I saw something that was both amazing and perplexing. I couldn't believe my eyes. There was Roscoe, or his ghost, standing there looking at me! I was so confused by this sight that I forgot I was supposed to run away. Instead, I stepped closer to see if this was really the old Roscoe. To my surprise, every time I took a step toward him, he took a step backward. Well, understanding flooded my mind so that I couldn't keep up with all the thoughts. But I knew one thing, I hadn't killed Roscoe, only knocked him unconscious; and something else, I stood up to a bully for the first time in my life. What a change! In the days and weeks to follow, Roscoe never attacked me again, and I learned that what I had been told was true, that underneath most bullies were like Roscoe, Just Chickens.

My mother's parents and siblings formed a tight group to the end and came quickly to each other's defense. And as long as grandma was alive there was an unwritten law; at holidays all would assemble in the Grand Ole House. I don't think the words "too many grandchildren," existed in her vocabulary. I remember Thanksgiving and Christmas meals that left us kids so full we would roll on the floor groaning in agony. Then two hours later we would be back picking at the leftovers. On Easter morning, families arrived with dozens of colored eggs and unseen baskets filled with candied eggs, yellow chicks and pink marshmallow rabbits. I remember a Fourth of July that came with a box that was reported to contain $10 worth of fireworks! It was full to overflowing and bristling with rockets, pinwheels, firecrackers, and smoke bombs. My cousin Richard, who is older and a little wiser in the ways of fireworks, allowed me to hold the firecracker while he lit the fuse. That was the summer I learned the literal meaning of "a short fuse." As I had stated earlier, leaving Minneapolis and moving out to the small town of Vancouver was a great adventure for me. I became a daily member of a wonderful new life surrounded by grandma and grandpa, orchards and gardens, exploring in the woodlands with my cousins and my very own dog named Penny. I should say here as well that grandpa was the only male figure in my growing up years. I learned a lot from grandpa, but it was more by osmosis, just being around him than direct tutelage. I went out with him on his sailboat many times, and he needed me because when the wind failed, I was his outboard motor that would get us back to the dock.

But the best was yet to come.

CHAPTER 7
THE FORTY-ACRE FARM

Normally good things come in bits and pieces, but in the early years things just got better and better. Somehow, I found myself living on a forty-acre farm, less than twenty miles north of grandma and grandpa's house. The community was called Ridgefield.

I have to come out of the vault for just a moment to say as an adult, this was a chronically impractical move on my mother's part. My mother, the dreamer, was a single woman; they were called divorcees back in the day. Mom was born and raised in the city of Minneapolis, and except for dogs, cats and rabbits, she had no experience with livestock. But she thought, "how hard could it be?"!!!

Mom had the good sense to lease the land out to a man who raised barley. But at one time this place out at the end of Kane Road had been a real working farm. Besides the house we lived in, there was an old orchard so covered with blackberry vines you couldn't get close to it. There was a commercial chicken house 200 feet long, a barn, a granary, corrals, and pig pens. For a ten-year-old boy it was heaven! There was simply no end to the exploration of these old buildings, and whoever created this odyssey threw nothing away. There were old farm implements here and there, pieces of iron thrown in piles, with wire, shovels, and forks with broken handles. Tools hung from rafters on rusty nails, tools that today you would only see in museums. These all needed to be investigated. Every can of nails, every box full of odds and ends, every shelf, and every Mason jar held treasures awaiting my discovery. Oh, the wonder of it all! Imagination; I had it in such abundance!

Not long after our arrival on the farm, mom started to assemble our own version of Old MacDonald's Farm. Lacking hands-on knowledge, she must have relied on scripture, because just like with Noah and the ark, all of our animals came two by two; two calves, two pigs, two horses, two sheep, etc. The two calves were jersey males not worth raising for meat, so the dairies would give them to feed stores, who in turn would give them to people like mom, providing she bought a bag of milk replacer to feed them. My sister's calf was named Ferdinand and became a large pet which we kept for years. I named my calf Hamburger. I don't think he cared much for the name, because he promptly scoured up and died late the next day. We put him in a little wagon and pulled him out of the barn for the night. The next morning, with shovel in hand, I discovered every part of Hamburger that was hanging over the side of the wagon, legs, tail, and ears had all been gnawed off by the coyotes. Well, it cut down on the digging.

Pigs are a must if you're going to have a bona-fide farm. They don't take much room. They produce a lot of meat. They are fun to watch and will eat just about anything, including leftovers. Our two pigs were named Daisy and Maisy, and they deserve special mention here. Not only did they eat all the yucky leftovers, but they also tried to eat my sister. It's true! She even missed a day of school once because they got loose and chased her across the barnyard and through the back porch, where she just barely got the back door shut in time to keep them out of the house. I would love to see a replay on that one someday. My sister received most of her DNA from our father. Things were either black or white, right or wrong with her. In her estimation, pigs were black. She never liked them, and I think the pigs could sense that and wanted her to get a closer look at them so she could see they were not so bad.

The real heavyweights on "happy acres" were the horses, Honey, a palomino Arabian mare, and her filly, Ho-Tif. Ho-Tif was completely and undeniably my sister's personal domain. She loved horses, and her earliest childhood dreams never wavered from the hope of having a horse of her own. That little filly was my sister's salvation. Through the hard years that followed, Ho- Tif was the only constant in her life, probably one of the few things she wouldn't change if she could. My brother, sister and I were all negatively affected in our own individual ways by the divorce of our parents, but none more so than my sister.

The Vault

Honey was mom's horse, but she never rode her. Mom explained that she would go riding once she got a saddle. She was true to her word. She never got a saddle, and she never rode her horse, not once. Because we had no saddle, I became a good rider at a young age. There was a real Hallmark moment that stands out because it was just so perfect. It had snowed a good two feet of dry, powdery snow, unusual for that part of Washington state. It was only a week or two before Christmas, so I decided to ride her out to a wooded area way out at the corner of the forty acres and find a tree. I used a small hatchet to cut down the perfect six-foot Christmas tree. Then with the hatchet and tree in my right hand I jumped on Honeys back, and we were off for home. What a picture that would have made, a young boy, a horse and a Christmas tree on that beautiful, sunny winter day. Honey must have sensed it was something special too, because she pranced like a show horse all the way home, with the dry snow billowing up around us.

Honey was a great kid's horse. She would put up with just about anything, and I have some happy memories here in the vault of the time my uncle Len came down from Alaska with his five kids. His eldest son Danny was my age, and we fell into mischief like we were born for it. One day we were riding Honey down a street near the farm, when we came to a side road that ended on our street. We crossed that OK. But when we got to the other side, instead of continuing down the side of the road, Honey stepped down into the ditch. Maybe because of the tall grass growing in the ditch, she didn't notice it was there or how deep it was. With her hind feet still on the road and her front feet way down in the bottom of the ditch, this put Honey's back at a forty-five-degree angle. We both tumbled off over her head into a tangle at her feet. We knew the only way for Honey to get out of this crazy mess was right over the top of us. The ditch was narrow, and it seemed the harder we wiggled to get apart and out of the horse's way, the more entangled we became. Meanwhile, that dear old horse just stood there in that awkward position, waiting until we finally managed to get out of her way. How hilarious we must have looked.

The next day we were back at it again. This time Danny wanted to try a solo ride. So, we got the bridle on Honey, and I took them out south of the barn where there was a hay field. It was ringed by woods on three sides, and our south fence on the fourth. There were no obstacles, just lots of nice soft, green grass in case he fell off. This would do fine. I helped him on her back, and gave him the basics on how to turn left and right, how to stop, and everything he needed to become a real horseman. I watched him as they started out, Danny slapping Honey's flanks with his bare feet, giving her rein. He was doing pretty good, but when they were about three-fourths of the way across the field, I saw Honey doing something I recognized as a potential problem. I thought, oh-oh! I forgot to tell him about that!

Honey was what you would call a barn horse. You had to boot her plenty to get her going away from the barn, but coming back was just the opposite. If you didn't hold her back, she would break out into a run. Also, if you weren't paying attention, she would slip in a three-degree turn that would slowly bring her back around toward the barn, because to her the barn meant quitting time. Well, I saw what she was up to and hollered at Danny to "rein her in hard," but they were too far away to hear me. Honey was making her three-degree turn back toward the barn and starting to speed up. You didn't need a keen eye to see things were on their way from bad to worse! Honey had completed her homeward turn, passing through a trot, on her way to an all-out run. I was surprised. Danny was doing a good job staying on her back. But the fence between them and the barn was fast approaching. Horse and rider parted company as she took a hard left, and Danny kept going right over the fence. The top of a steel fence post caught the cuff of one pant leg and ripped his britches almost clean off! Funny thing is that he came out of it with hardly a scratch!

You never know on the day that it happens that you are making a happy memory. Today might turn out to be the best day of your life, because you don't know where tomorrow is going to take you. Moms "I'll ride my horse when I get a saddle" became to me a syndrome of something we often find ourselves doing, putting off hope and happiness until some requirement is met, like getting some position in life, getting out of debt, or finding the right person. Money and possessions don't make you happy. Happiness comes on a day you least expect it. So,

watch for it, because right now today could become "the good old days."

Danny and I had a wonderful handful of days on that visit. A few years later in 1968, that handsome young man came to a day he did not know would take away his life, killed in a car crash.

CHAPTER 8
HAYSEED AND THE WATERING HOLE

There was a watering hole for livestock out east of the buildings. A spring had been dug out into a small pond. It wasn't very big around, maybe sixty or seventy feet across, but it was quite deep. On hot summer days, it was a great place to cool off. The water was muddy, about the color of coffee with a bit of cream, but this was something easily overlooked by small boys.

One day a boy we called Hayseed had come down to go swimming with me. He was the son of the man who grew barley on our forty acres, and lived on the other end of Kane Road. He was not the sharpest tool in the drawer to be sure, but he was big, and a lot stronger than I was. I don't recall seeing him dressed in anything other than bib overalls, a straw hat, and bare feet. I think it was my sister who came up with the name "Hayseed." He didn't like to be teased, or the nickname, so our usual activities together involved him chasing me for all he was worth, cussing and threatening what he would do to me when he caught me, which he never did. I could run like a deer. But this day was too hot for running and his overalls and straw hat lay on the bank next to my clothes. I dove into the coffee-colored pond and swam under the water to the other bank. I surfaced just in time to see Hayseed's bellyflop into the middle of the pond.

I've seen in my own life and the lives of other people that great calamity comes on days when vital information is missing. On that particular day, there were two things that would have been helpful to know; number one, I didn't know that "Hayseed" couldn't swim a lick, and number two, "Hayseed" didn't know that the water he was jumping into was over nine feet deep!

Hayseed breached like a great whale, bellering for help and flopping his big arms on the water as if he could beat it into submission. I thought he was fooling around. But then he was gone, replaced by a big eruption of bubbles. It's hard to make the transition from a fun summer day to the comprehension of disaster. When he surfaced again, he was coughing out water and gasping for air, and then he went down again. It was then that I realized this is what it looks like to drown! It comes with no warning, no time to think. It took only a second to swim over to him, and it was my intention to pull him to the shallows at the bank. But when I got hold of him, he got hold of me, and in his panic, there was no reasoning with him. He frantically grabbed me, pushed me down to the bottom of the pond, and tried to secure a purchase on top of my head. I could feel the mud on the bottom of the pond squishing up through my toes and around my ankles, and I knew this was now my disaster too! He was too strong for me, and I couldn't get away. Time was running out for both of us. It could have all ended right there in that little coffee-colored pond. Somewhere on the third or fourth page of the local newspaper, a headline would read "accidental drowning kills two boys." It would go on to tell that the boys reported missing the night before were found early the next morning by a deputy sheriff.

But it didn't end there. With my lungs burning and about to burst, I did the only thing that came to mind. I let go of what little air I had and swam for the bottom. It worked! When his life preserver became a rock, he let go and I was free. Even then, I barely made it to the surface without gulping huge lungs full of water. Weakly, I crawled out on the bank and found an old branch I could use as a lifeline to pull him in to safety.

We never went swimming again, and I don't recall him ever threatening to beat me up either! But I learned a big lesson that day and in the long years since I have seen a number of people jump into a disastrous relationship, get underwater financially or just make bad lifelong decisions. They drowned, because in their panic there is no reasoning with them.

CHAPTER 9
ADOLF HITLER'S MEANER BROTHER

I'm thinking back to that little boy I once was, the mama's boy, the believer, the one who never caught on that it was his mom who was pulling the tubes out of the television set. I'm reveling in the memories of those early years in Washington, grandma and grandpa, the farm, the animals, my dog Penny, and all the happy memories that exist in the vault. Looking around though, I see darker colors in the part that comes next. Over the next few years that little believer, that mama's boy, would cease to exist. It all started when a man no one knew showed up one day at the farm selling vacuum cleaners. I think he was friends with the old man Kane next door for whom our road was named. I don't know what my mother's motivation could have been; was it really love, was it physical needs, or had she simply gotten lonely? But in June of 1961 my mother married that man who would terrorize all of our lives for the next four years. His name was Herb, and it turns out that he was a bonafide schizophrenic, you never knew from day to day, even from moment to moment who you would be dealing with,

Dr. Jekyll or Mr. Hyde. I remember one evening the three of us were eating dinner together. Just for fun Herb reached across the table, got some butter on his knife, and passed it by mother's face, dabbing butter on her nose. Not to be outdone mother picked up the butter dish and pushed it in Herb's face. She ran off laughing for the bathroom and locked herself in. In this moment of hilarity which he created, he turned into the beast that we would all come to know over the next few years. He kicked the bathroom door so hard that he broke the entire door casing lose from the wall along with the door, pushing the whole thing two feet into the bathroom.

I was fourteen years old in 1962. It seemed that no one noticed that I was failing in school, had a horribly low self-esteem, and carried a growing "bag" of regrets. I was alone in my troubles, and more than that, I felt whatever happened good or bad, I somehow had it coming. I could barely read or write. How a person learned to spell words was an absolute mystery to me, (common in people with dyslexia). In the year of my seventh grade, I had missed over twenty days of school, and never did I hear a word from home or school officials about it. Way to go Covington Junior High!! In the fall of 1962, in spite of failing the seventh grade, I started the eighth grade. I didn't fit in with kids my age. I had no close friends. School was awful, and home was getting worse. If I had someone to confide in, I wouldn't have said a word, because it would never have entered my mind that I had a right to. For example, my bedroom was in an unfinished, unheated attic of the old house we were living in. All I had for blankets was one of those thin wool army blankets. I would get so cold that I used to take a light bulb on a cord under the blanket so it could warm me up. But then I would fall asleep and the light would burn a hole in the blanket. I never said a word. To make matters worse there was a second bedroom downstairs that mom kept made-up for my sister just in case she ever decided to come home. I think that bed had an electric blanket on it.

There were unseen troubles ahead, disaster for me was right around the corner. I was riding my bike after school with this kid named Ricky. Because I knew Herb was at the house, I was in no hurry to get home, so we rode over to the elementary school, just for something to do. We were having what people called "dog days." That's when summer seemed to linger on and on into fall. You could smell the skunk weed growing in the ditch on the side of the road. It was a warm, lazy, quiet afternoon. We rode side by side so we could talk, though I have no idea what we talked about. I do remember him telling me that a car was coming up behind us. I couldn't hear the car so I must've assumed it was a long way behind us. At any rate I was the one closest to the center line, which meant I needed to move. I had three options, and any physicist would agree that I chose the right one, from an energy standpoint, that is. I could have slowed down and pulled in behind Ricky, but that would have resulted in the loss of inertia, a precious commodity on a hot day. I also had the option of increasing my speed, allowing me to pull over in front of Ricky. There is a formula that states something to the effect that it takes X units of energy to move X amount of matter over X amount of distance. Well, I couldn't have done the math, and as I said, these were "dog days." What was needed here was a third option, something that required less resistance. An old adage comes to mind that says "men and rivers both become crooked by taking the path of least resistance." I was about to get crooked. Then the solution came to me. Since I was already so close to the center of the road, I could just move over a few feet to the left side, and let the car pass between Ricky and myself. What an elegant solution! I surprised myself - and a lot of other people too. I'm sure Ricky was impressed with my idea, because just like that, I was snatched from his side and deposited in a broken heap 300 feet down the road in less time than it takes to say "holy cow!"

About a month and a half later, I started getting flashbacks about the instant before the "big bang," when the moveable and immoveable objects met, just quick glimpses of the hood and the front bumper. I could have reached out and touched it, but all I had time for was to grip the handlebars, close my eyes, and grit my teeth, because this was really going to hurt. I went over the hood and through the windshield. I would like to see Evil Kanievel beat that. Jumping over cars is a lot easier than going through them. When the woman driving the car slammed on her brakes, I was ejected back out through the broken windshield and must have caught on something that flung me up into the air. It was in Ricky's testimony that if I had been another ten feet to the side, I would have landed in the telephone wires. He did have the best seat in the house. The police estimated, based on her testimony and the 240 feet of skid marks, that her speed at the point of impact was sixty miles per hour.

Family members had to take turns sitting with me twenty-four hours a day for the first week. My entire head was wrapped in gauze bandages and I guess I had kept trying to pull them off. I had received 147 stitches in just my face alone. The heavy chrome bumper had crushed both bones just above my left ankle. I was in critical condition because of the extensive loss of blood, so they didn't work on my leg, only stabilized it for the first two weeks. They performed surgery on my leg and inserted a steel plate. That hurt worse than anything. But I am thankful to Dr. Osborn. He did a great job. I had to have a full-length cast on that leg for a year and a half. But he got the foot on straight, and it has given me almost no trouble at all. Several plastic surgery operations gave me back what could pass for my old face. Kids can be so sweet. I remember one of them told me it looked like my face had caught on fire and someone tried to put it out with a fire axe. It actually seems a little funny now.

I spent a month in the hospital, and after the pain from my leg surgery subsided, I was given a brand-new chrome wheelchair. This was a big mistake on the part of the hospital, because in a matter of days, I became a master of the chair. I could go the full length of the hall, balancing on my back wheels. I had been moved to a 14-bed ward at the end of the hall. My bed was to the right, just inside the door. I would go barreling flat out down the hall toward my room. As soon as I would pass the door, I would yank on my right brake, locking up that wheel. The chair would spin violently around and slap right up against my bed. All of this was being done with a full-length plaster cast that stuck out from the chair like a battering ram. Everyone seemed guardedly amused with my exploits in the chair, everyone except the janitor. There were black skid marks appearing all up and down the halls, and the closer you got to my room, the more concentrated they became, ending in a sharp J hook at the side of my bed.

I was having fun, but it was about to end. I don't know if all Catholic hospitals were built in the shape of a cross, but St. Joe's was. Four hallways met at the center of the cross. That is where I was destined to meet my "wheelchair Waterloo." I had been out touring in my chair. The smooth linoleum floor and the hard black rubber wheels were made for speed. I came to the intersection flat out and pulled on my left brake, intending to head down my hall. Instead, I ran slap-smack into a Med Nurse, the end of my heavy plaster cast catching her in the midsection. I heard a Whoosh as the air was expelled from her lungs, and she went flying backward to the floor. The med tray she carried contained dozens of tiny paper cups, each one carefully marked and filled with the appropriate drugs. It went straight up in the air, and then came down with a loud clatter on the linoleum floor. Pills went rolling off in every direction. Those narrow-minded nuns replaced my chair with an old, squeaky, wood and wicker chair that must have been left over from the Spanish-American War! The drive wheels were way out front, with those wobbly wheels in back, top speed two-and-a-half miles per hour. I was starting to feel like a cripple.

Mom gave me a black & white TV up in my attic bedroom, so for the rest of that school year and the next I watched the Steve Allen Show. I learned an important lesson about going up and down stairs on crutches; always step down with the crutches first, then down with the cast; crutches first, then the cast. I tried stepping down with the cast one time, and found myself hanging in space with the crutches in my armpits. I did a complete somersault to the bottom of the steps, where the heel of my cast made a hole in the door about five-and-a-half feet up.

In 1962, I was the only kid left in the house. My stepbrother Dale, who I really liked, had joined the army, my brother had gone into the Air Force, and my sister ran away with the circus. My sister hated Herb, for good reason, and this was her only way out. My brother left me with a fairly good guitar with six strings. I am sure glad that he did, because the guitar has become one of my best life-long friends. It always knows exactly how I feel, and faithfully harmonizes with my every mood. But that guitar wouldn't last long.

One night around 10:00 p.m. Herb came into the kitchen. It must have been in the winter because it was very dark. He was alone. But then mom came in, and she looked awful, both eyes were blackened, and her lips puffed up and her dentures were broken. Herb said they had been in an accident; they didn't hit anything but when he slammed on the brakes her face had hit the dashboard and that's what did the damage. Two weeks later my sister told me the truth, that Herb had beat her up with his bare fists. About a month later the same thing happened. Herb came in the kitchen door late at night all by himself. That's when I smarted off and asked Herb if he had beat my mom up again. Mother came in the house just in time to see Herb deliver one of his South-Forty Haymakers that sent me, plaster cast and all, flying across the living room into the middle of the couch, which cracked in two on impact. Mom was starting to get her fill of this man. She grabbed the first thing she could lay her hands on, My Guitar, and swung it down for all she was worth on top of Herb's head. "El Ka-bong!!" I saw the whole thing from my heap on the couch. It is kind of funny the thoughts that went through my mind. I saw the split run up the face of the guitar when it made contact with his head and thought, "maybe it can still be fixed." But then Herb grabbed it from her, threw it down on the floor, and jumped up and down on it like a big ape. I thought, "no, probably not now!" I think we used it for kindling.

Mom was married and divorced one more time while I was still in the house. If that wasn't enough, she was married and divorced a fourth time later in life. I sound kind of mean here and I guess I shouldn't, because someday my kids are probably going to write about what I did that was so annoying to them.

I wasn't mean, nor was I any kind of a rebel. I was completely lacking directions. When I was with bad people I did bad things, when I was with good people, I did good things. I was like a ship that had slipped its moorings, drifting in and out of precarious waters, oblivious to the dangers. In gale force winds with nary a sail furled, I plunged mindlessly through those early years. Be it drugs or alcohol, potentially disastrous relationships, and the worst of company, I sailed the good ship giddy idiot. Looking back now, there were many times I came so close to ruination. Mother had this problem with relationships. I get that, but so did her siblings and companions of the time. It was a new thing; everybody was getting divorced back then. But in-between making our lives miserable, she gave me something of great value.

On my eighteenth birthday she gave me my first leather-bound, onion-leafed Bible, with my name gold embossed. I still have it. She started me out on something that has given me a lifetime of blessing. Mother told me that there were thirty-one days in over half the months of the year, and there were thirty-one chapters in the book of Proverbs. She said whatever day it was, say the seventeenth, then read the seventeenth chapter, and if you fall behind, (I was always falling behind), don't try to make it up. If it's the twenty-fourth, then read the twenty-fourth chapter. She never said anything about stopping, so as of today's writing, I have been reading Proverbs for fifty-six years. There are many books in the Bible that tell you what to do, but Proverbs is the only book that tells you how to do it. I have avoided many life-changing wrong decisions based on Proverbs, and I have made many right decisions over my lifetime. For example, when a certain young girl came into my life, I knew right away that she was the right one because I had been reading about her for three or four years in the book of Proverbs. And further, through that little girl God has restored unto me all the years that the locust had eaten.

By the way, at the time of this writing we just celebrated our fiftieth wedding anniversary.

CHAPTER 10
Daniel Boone

You have to understand the gravity of the adventure that lay before me early in the spring of 1970. My '65 Ford pickup was outfitted with a homemade plywood canopy. Inside were all the essentials: A motorcycle, assorted tools, a few changes of clothes, a bedroll, a fifty-five-gallon drum of gas, and a six-foot siphon hose. I figured the wad of $5 and $10 bills in my pocket was sufficient for the 800 miles to Vanderhoof, British Columbia. That is where mom's baby brother, my Uncle Len, was making a desperate attempt to get a sawmill up and running. I had worked in a sawmill, knew how to weld and use a cutting torch, and I was going to help. In those days, the direction of my life changed as often as the weather in Vancouver, Washington. So, throwing my outfit together and heading north was no big deal. It was going to be an adventure.

Uncle Len was the family favorite, partly I suppose because he was living his father's dream of being a pioneer. Grandpa favored the American Indians and the early pioneers. He often lamented that he was born 100 years too late. Len moved to Alaska in 1955, America's last frontier. Tales told of his exploits as a story teller, hunter, explorer, woodsman and a survivor, rivaled that of Daniel Boone. Mother was proud of her baby brother, and why not? He was a handsome, well-built man. As a matter of fact, he did resemble Fes Parker, the Hollywood star who played Daniel Boone in the Walt Disney movies. He had the same penetrating eyes that lock onto you, not in a malevolent way, but like he was focusing all of his attention on you. It made you feel like what you had to say was important to him. He was and is a good storyteller, with an endearing, self-effacing sense of humor that always pulled you into his corner.

I never missed an episode of Daniel Boone, and I used to read stories about mountain men and dreamed that I would one day be like them. I was just like my grandpa wishing that I was born 100 years earlier. I taught myself to throw a double bitted axe, and I got to where I could always hit my mark on a tree or a chunk of firewood. I became very good with a bullwhip, an absolute must for a good mountain man. There are five tips on a Maple Leaf, and I could snap off one tip at a time with my bullwhip and never miss. I remember uncle Len being down for a visit and he was over at our house, so I had showed him what I could do with a bullwhip. He was pretty impressed. I made the mistake of saying I could pick the ash off the end of his cigarette with my whip. Then uncle Len, aka Daniel Boone, fished a cigarette out of his pack, lit it up and stuck it in his mouth, and waited for me to do what I said I could do. I told him if I happened to miss, I could take his eye out, so I made him hold it out in his hand instead.

Len was the toughest man I had ever known, or at least tried to put on a show that he was. On cold mornings when everyone else was buttoned up to the chin, he would be standing bare-headed, coat hanging open, and grinning like it was the finest of days. I think his motto should have been "when it was too tough for everyone else, it was just right for Len." He went through a string of devastating losses and set-backs that would have left the average man broken. Len had dreamed of owning land, lots of it, land he could farm and raise cattle on. It was a dream a long time in the making. With what was in 1965 a good bit of money saved, he moved his family to Vanderhoof, BC. But there were unseen troubles ahead, like the iceberg waiting silently for the Titanic. In the span of a few short years their marriage was over, the money gone, and the dream was dead. If that wasn't bad enough, they lost their oldest son, Danny, in a car crash. But Len served a God of mercy, for out of the ashes and against all odds his dream was revived and achieved. Len found a deepening sense of humility that marked the man for the rest of his life. ***I believe there are some things in life that can only be learned through suffering.***

Most important, my Uncle Len was and is a God Seeker. Today, if you engage him in spiritual matters, you would find his responses come in halting, clipped phrases, using his hands and facial expressions, looking for the perfect description, as if words were not well suited to express his thoughts and feelings about God. Somewhere in the long, hard years of his life, he found peace with God, and something we should all be looking for, humility.

He excelled at turning a most miserable situation into an adventure. I remember a time my wife Millie and I were with Len in our car. He was showing us some really beautiful lakes, directing us down roads more suited to a jeep than our two-wheel drive Chevy Vega. We came to a low spot that looked really muddy, but Len assured me we could make it through, which we did. Driving only another two to three hundred feet past the mud hole he had us stop. We got out and walked a short distance to a third lake. It was beautiful, but I'm thinking, why didn't we just stop on the other side of the muddy spot and walk the two hundred feet? Well sure enough going back through that wet spot we got stuck, and I mean stuck good. It became obvious that the only way we were going to get out of there was to build a cord wood road. Well neither one of us happened to have a chainsaw in our back pocket, so finding the right pieces of wood to stick under the wheels to get us out of there was a real chore. It took us two hours to leverage that car up onto polls, all the time uncle Len was jabbering on about this and that, like he was having the time of his life. Well, we were ready. Len and I had polls to pry against the back bumper. Millie hopped into the driver seat, and Len told her once the car got moving "don't take your foot off the gas for nothing!" I wish we had a video of what happened next. Len said "go," we pushed as hard as we could on the polls, and Millie put the peddle to the metal! And it was hilarious; a rooster tail of mud shot out forty feet from both tires all the way up the hill! Of course, Len and I were covered with mud, and he just laughed and laughed. Millie did just what he told her, she kept her foot on the gas, fishtailing and throwing mud all the way to the top of the hill.

Len was showing me around his farm one day and we came to a place where he had about six beehives. I told him about a time when I was just a little kid, getting stung by a bunch of bumblebees that were in a nest in the ground. I was stung six or seven times and it had scared me something awful. I told him I was still afraid of bees. Then my uncle did something that both surprised and amazed me. He started telling me about how wonderful bees were and that they had very predictable personalities. He said, "Look at today for example; it's warm and sunny, and there's plenty of nectar coming into the hive. This makes the bees very docile." At the same time that he is telling me this, he walks right up to a hive, with his bare hands he removes the lid and then the inner lid from one of the hives. I could see hundreds and hundreds of bees crawling around inside the top of the hive. Then he carefully removed one of the frames and gently lifted it out of the hive, careful not to hurt any of the bees. It was covered with worker bees filling both sides of the frame with honey. Then he held the frame in his left hand, and with his right hand, I kid you not, he stroked the bees as if he were petting them. Each time his hand went over the frame, the bees made a sound like, "varoom,

varoom." He carefully replaced the frame back into the hive and put the lids back in place. I was transfixed and amazed by what I had seen. My uncle, along with all his other attributes, was also a bee charmer! My fear of bees was replaced by amazement that day, and it wasn't long before I was keeping bees myself.

At the time, my desire to be of help to this venerated uncle was totally genuine, but I wonder how Uncle Len viewed this "help" that was presently thundering up the rugged Fraser River Canyon toward Vanderhoof. Now so many years later, I am too big of a chicken to come straight out and ask him, but I'm afraid the notion of me coming to help was greeted with some trepidation, like asking Dr. Kevorkian to assist the medical team for your upcoming heart transplant.

The fifty-five-gallon drum was intended to save money. Gas was cheaper in the US. I was hoping to get most of the way without buying the more expensive Canadian gas. The guy who sold me the drum said it had an added benefit of containing fifteen gallons of white gas, which would burn just fine when mixed with regular gasoline. He was a nice fellow. My brother had come along for the ride and to help do some of the driving. We stopped at mid-afternoon at a small café in Hope, British Columbia. After we ate, I filled the truck using the siphon hose. We hadn't made it out of that small town when for no particular reason that Ford just up and died. No amount of coaxing, cranking, or cursing would bring her back to life. So, we pushed it back to a garage in town. The mechanic said he would try to get to it later, but not to expect anything until morning. After ham and eggs, we walked over to the shop and found the mechanic sitting at the front desk, smoking a hand-rolled cigarette. We asked him how things were going with the Ford, expecting to hear the worst. He removed his cigarette with a greasy hand and blew smoke across the cluttered desk. I didn't like his grin. It suggested words I really didn't want to hear, like "you dummy" or "you idiot." "Boys," he said, "your truck is running fine, that is after I drained about ten gallons of water off of the bottom of your tank!" Come to think of it, that nice fellow who sold me the drum containing "white gas" had a smile just like that. So much for saving money! We pulled out onto highway 1, heading north up the Fraser River, dodging frost boils all the way.

We arrived in Vanderhoof road-weary and worn. The old pickup had burped now and then when bits of water found its way to the carburetor. But it was mostly over its indigestion and sat cooling in Uncle Len's front yard. He had built his own house, or half of it, which was long on idea but short on cash. It stood with a shed roof facing the road, the other half missing, waiting on better times. It was "rusticated," complete with an outhouse. But it was warm, well built, and sat there patiently waiting for paint. Running water came in buckets lugged up from a spring in the gully.

Len had remarried a local gal. Her name was Muriel. The two of them seemed to fit together like peas and carrots. She had no problem doing without modern conveniences like hot and cold running water or refrigeration. As long as they had each other, it seemed they could weather any storm. Len had four kids and Muriel three, so I made number ten. It reminds me of the old song, "Poor Folks."

There was ten of us a liven' in a two-room shack on the banks of the river by the railroad tracks.

It would have simplified bath time if their place had been on the river. It took four to five trips uphill from the spring with a five-gallon bucket in each hand. Then the water had to be heated on the gas stove in metal buckets. Everyone washed in the same water. By the time we were all through, you could have planted corn in it. It gives you the idea of how the old expression "don't throw the baby out with the bath water" came to be. The water got so dirty by the time you got to the baby; you couldn't see them.

There were more than just people in that little house. Muriel, that slender Canadian Rose who could bloom in the poorest of soils had one obsession: Cats, a whole gang of them, and their leader was a low-down, sneaky Siamese cat named Spitinella. These cats never used the floor. They could circumnavigate the house via the chest of drawers, countertops, table, washing machine, bookcase, etc., and never touch the floor. I was standing there at the counter making a peanut butter and jelly sandwich, and here came Spitinella just as pretty as you please, right through the middle of my fixins. She gave her tail a flick right under my nose as if to dismiss me as a lower life form. I turned and looked at Muriel, who was watching what I would do. She gave me a look that said "don't even think it!"

I know some would think me a cat hater, but it just isn't so. Be reasonable; if you made a side-by-side comparison of mankind's two favorite pets, the dog comes out on top every time. Just ask yourself, if your kid is drowning, who will jump in and save him, a cat or a dog? If you shoot a duck, who will go bring it back, a cat or a dog? If you stumble across a bull moose in rut, who will keep him occupied while you shinny up a tree, a cat or a dog? See what I mean? There is no comparison. They write songs about dogs. "The Cat Came Back" is the only song I know about cats, and in that song, they are trying to get rid of the dang thing! And where is the cat counterpart to Lassie, Rin-Tin-Tin, or Old Yeller? Face it; to a dog you are a god, to a cat you are staff, or at best a royal subject.

The cats ate better than we did by far. Muriel's trips to the store always produced the same goods: two loaves of white bread, six cans of evaporated milk, six cans of cat food, and one can of Spam to split among whoever showed up for dinner. It is not that I mean to complain, but after a while that cat food started looking pretty good.

The day after I arrived, we went out to see the sawmill Len and his friend had been working on. I was amazed at what had been accomplished. It was truly ingenious and desperate at the same time. There was a humorous saying from my days in the Portland shipyards that came to mind as I surveyed that scene. "*We the unwilling, being led by the unqualified, have been doing the unbelievable for so long with so little, we now attempt the impossible with nothing!"* The day I arrived, work on the mill itself was on hold so they could replace a broken mainspring in a large caterpillar. The spring was being replaced with a rigid steel box frame, presumably to save time and money. There was an old Pettibone loader used to lift logs up to the deck of the mill. The lifting forks could be extended six to eight feet out in front of itself. The lift arms were hinged clear to the back end of the loader. It was huge and lumbering, and looked like a bony dinosaur. At one time, it was a state-of-the-art loader, four-wheel drive and four-wheel steering. But now it was crippled with age and a lack of preventative maintenance. Only one set of wheels turned by then, and the original power plant had been replaced with a small Chevy six-cylinder engine. It was morosely under-powered. I think top speed was less than two to three miles per hour, and with its crippled steering it wallowed in the mud like a doomed mastodon in a tar pit.

The saw mill itself was pretty impressive in design and application. It was a gang saw, which could cut a whole tree at once. The power plant was the family car, a Buick, a '58, I think. They had parked it horizontal to the in-feed deck, removed the right rear wheel, and with a torch cut the hub out of that wheel. Then they attached a drive line that powered the mill to the hub and reattached it to the Buick. Dang, it worked! They had run a few logs through, enough to know that the Buick was geared too high. The rear end of the drive had to go, but how? To pull the motor and transmission out, and then weld together a frame to mount it on would have taken days. They didn't have days. The bank was poised to repossess anything of value. Then I suggested we cut the Buick in half. That would get rid of the differential but leave the motor and transmission in its old mounts. Say good-bye to the family car. I cut off both front doors, cut the roof, the floor, and then the frame. We picked up our new, improved power plant with the Pettibone, and pointed the tail shaft of the tranny toward the mill. We needed badly to saw a few thousand feet of lumber just to show the banker we had a going concern here. Since the car had an automatic transmission, we didn't have to concern ourselves with clutch or gear shift, but we needed some kind of linkage from the carburetor up to the deck where the operator would stand. Here entered the fatal flaw. I suggested that we run a wire from a control handle on the deck to the carburetor, reverse the spring on the carburetor so it pulled open, and the wire would hold it back. We finished all of the final odds and ends, and were looking forward to our first day of sawing logs. There is a lot more that should be said about the ingenuity built into that mill, but in the end it didn't matter.

Early the next morning, we were half way through our first log. The heavy gang saw going up and down was cutting perfectly. It was also shaking the deck pretty good. Hindsight is 20/20, and any one of us should have seen this coming. There was a number of agonizingly simple ways to prevent the catastrophe that was seconds away from happening. The shaking deck loosened the handle and allowed the spring on the carburetor to pull the throttle wide open. Uncle Len was closest to the throttle when the whole saw mill went ballistic. The big Buick V8 ran the mill nicely at a fast idle, so when the throttle popped open, the whole operation jumped into warp drive. It took Len precious seconds to realize what had happened and get to the faulty throttle control. If you were the sort to believe in fate, you would conclude it was not smiling on us that day, nor would we get a second chance to get things right. The mill was broken and broken bad. The heavy cast iron casing was cracked on both sides, and the 6-inch steel drive shaft was twisted. The mill was history.

Then I witnessed the most amazing thing. In less than forty minutes, Uncle Len/Daniel Boone was forming a new plan. There was no more sawmill, so he was getting himself set to be a logger, start dropping trees to send to the big mill in town. He didn't cry, he didn't cuss, and he didn't blame anybody. Of course, I blamed myself. The thing with the throttle was my idea. I'm okay with it now because I see a bigger picture was being fashioned in our lives. In spite of all of the frustrations he was going through at the time, Uncle Len came out a winner.

I continued working with Len on projects around the farm, building fence and clearing land. I had applied for a permanent residency in Canada and was waiting for my work visa. The weather was warming up, so I thought I would strike out on my own, get out of that crowded cabin.

Daniel Boone

I moved my pickup out into the woods and parked it next to the mill. There was of course no electricity, running water, or bathroom. But there were no people to run into either. I had a bedroll under the home-made canopy where I slept, and there was an old truck rim I rolled over a fire to use for a stove. What else did I need? I had made friends with some guys in town, and my guitar got me invited to parties and get-togethers. I went back and forth to town on the motorcycle I brought up with me. Back then, they had a law against having handlebars higher than eighteen inches above the tank. Mine were about twenty-four. One day I got pulled over by a Mountie in Vanderhoof. He was large. He got out of his patrol car with a tape measurer in one hand, and swaggered over to me in a kind of chubby Clint Eastwood style. He had this look about him that said "All right you smart aleck little *$#@*%*#, I've got you now!" He didn't know it, but I was ready for him. I kept the bolts on the "dog bones" (that's the part that holds the handle-bars) just a little bit loose. When he pulled out his tape, I pulled the handlebars right down to the tank. He bellered at me to put them back up. So, I did, about half-way up. I give him credit for being smart enough to know he lost that round. He put his tape away and extracted my license and proof of insurance. He walked across the street to the police department hoping to get something on me there, which he didn't. Good thing for me that there were no computers back then or he would have discovered I had written and cancelled my liability insurance to get badly needed cash.

The Vault

I got back out to the mill after dark one night, and after my ears got over the racket of the motorcycle, I started hearing something. I couldn't make out what it was. I almost had myself convinced that it was just my imagination, because it seemed to go away. But then there it was back again, louder. I walked around the mill in the moonlight trying to get a sense of which direction the sound was coming from. But that seemed to be changing too. First, I heard it from the north, and then it seemed to be coming from the east. Then it dawned on me that the sound was a little bit like steam escaping from a hot engine. "That's it," I thought. Some kids have been horsing around with some of the equipment. But when I had felt all of the radiators, I found they were as cold as stone. "Now ain't this getting a little bit creepy," I thought, out here in the middle of the woods, just me and this unidentifiable buzzing sound. Old re-runs of "The Twilight Zone" and "The Outer Limits" were popping into my mind, offering bizarre explanations for this phenomenon. With the hair starting to stand up on the back of my neck, I crawled up on the deck of the sawmill. I stood there listening. It was maddening; every direction I turned my head I could hear the sound. "Oh, this is it" I thought, "the aliens are finally landing!" I happened to look up, and what I saw was worse than aliens. It was mosquitoes, millions and millions of them! I have never seen anything like it before or since. It must have been a pocket of warm air that held a cloud of mosquitoes twenty feet thick and as far as I could see in every direction. The bottom of the cloud was as flat as a table top, about ten feet over my head. I thought about what I might look like in the morning if I were the only thing out here for them to eat. I hung a tarp over the back of my canopy, lit two or three mosquito coils, and zipped my sleeping bag all the way up to my neck. I think I dreamt about the movie "The Birds" by Alfred Hitchcock.

CHAPTER 11
SPITNELLA AND THE T-BONE

I still didn't have a permit from the Canadian Government to work, so I took a job picking roots. In the '60s, people in British Columbia couldn't sell their trees, so they pushed them up in big windrows and burned them. The fertile land under the trees was worth more than the forest. I was the equivalent of the present-day wet-back here in the US. I was doing work the Canadians wouldn't do, picking roots and branches between the windrows so the land could be planted in pasture. With my first paycheck, I bought food. Hallelujah! A whole box full! I put it under the deck of the sawmill for safe keeping. I came in from town the next day, hungry, but for the first time in several weeks I knew there was food waiting, so I was happy. I was about to learn a lesson. When living in the wild, don't ever take food for granted. A bear, or possibly a wolverine had found my box, torn it open, and eaten everything, even biting open cans of soup. The only thing left was one white onion. As a parting gesture, whatever it was pooped all over my home-made stove! I went to bed hungry for the first time in my life because I had no food. I had been hungry lots of times, all the time, but there was always something to eat, a meal waiting somewhere, but not then. I think it is strange today in a world where there is so much hunger, that a twenty-one-year-old could experience hunger, real hunger for the first time in his life.

I brooded around camp the next morning, not knowing what to do with this growling thing in my gut. Finally, I thought of my uncle's place. At least I knew there would be cat food there. I walked overland through the woods to Len's house. I found there was no one home except for the cats. They must have sensed my hunger. They watched my every move as I came into the kitchen. Then I saw on the gas stove a left-over pot of oatmeal. My stomach did an "Oh for Joy" double-back flip at the sight of that pot! I turned on the gas and poured in some canned milk and sugar. Wow! It ranks up there with the ten best meals of my life!

Revived and regrouped, I recounted my woes to a good friend in town named Sven, who worked at the bar in the hotel. I was a regular at the bar mostly because of a policy they had on a drink called "a zombie." It contained seven different kinds of liquors and was in a large tumbler the size of an ice tea glass. It seems really dumb to me now, but the deal was if you could drink three zombies and still be able to get up and walk out of the bar, you didn't have to pay for them. Over all the months I spent in Vanderhoof

Spitnella And The T-Bone

I never paid for a single drink. Some people are gifted in that way. I think I get it from my dad, he was Irish.

Now Sven being the Good Samaritan that he was, took my plight to heart and promptly stole a T-bone steak from the cooler at the restaurant. I took it as an international expression of good will between two great nations. God Bless Them Canadians! Now, I couldn't risk cooking this precious steak on my old pooped-on stove out at the mill, so I waited until I knew my aunt and uncle would be out of the house. I didn't want to be answering any questions about how a poor spam-eating Yankee boy came to be in possession of such a fine slab of beef.

I walked into the house and there were cats! Cats on the countertop, cats by the door, cats on the bookcase, cats on the floor, each pair of eyes riveted on what was in my right hand, the steak. They must have smelled it before I even got in the house. Just to make sure, I waved the steak from left to right in front of me. Each head wagged back and forth in time with the meat. It reminded me of the old kitchen clocks with the black and white face of a cat, its eyes and tail ticking back and forth like a pendulum. I don't care how small they were, to be the focused object of this little band of carnivores felt a little bit freaky! I envisioned myself fighting my way through a blizzard of feral cats on the way to the frying pan. I stamped my foot and hollered, breaking the spell and sending cats milling about the house with their tails twitching in anticipation. "This is not going to be easy," I thought. They had no refrigerator. There was no safe place to put the meat down while I readied the pan. Then my eyes fell on the old wringer washing machine beside the door. I walked over and lifted the round lid. It was empty. It was clean. It had to be safe. I deposited the steak inside the washer and carefully replaced the lid.

Smiling at my ingenuity, I started preparing the pan. As I sliced onion into the melting butter, I looked over my right shoulder at the washer. The cats seemed to have lost interest. Well, that was fine. I took my time, added salt and pepper. Keeping one eye on the washer, I sautéed those onions to opaque perfection. My empty belly was gurgling and growling like it was full of aliens, but I took my time, reveling in the glory of the meal to come. Finally, I burrowed a hole in the onions to make room for my beautiful steak. How long had it been since I had a real piece of meat? Two, three months, I don't remember. But all was well. Today, I was going to eat. I slipped happily over to the washer and lifted the lid, and there was –

Ahhhh! Oh My Gosh! I couldn't believe my eyes!

There was that demonic feline, Spitinella, with my steak. She was going after it like she was a chain saw! When the lid lifted and the light flooded in, she rolled one evil eye up at me, and then redoubled her efforts, gobbling up the entire tenderloin half of the T-bone.

Spitnella And The T-Bone

Caution!

Small children and cat lovers should leave the room now. You don't want to hear what I am about to do to that naughty putty tat!!!

She knew she was caught, knew punishment would be swift and terrible, yet she continued defiantly gulping mouthfuls of steak, right up to the instant my fingers closed like a vise around her miserable little throat. I stomped out through the door with Spitinella, her eyes bulging in the death grip of my right hand. A youth within my prime, with Hell's own fury, I heaved Spitinella for all I was worth into the gully behind the house. If it had been a football instead of a cat, she would have made it into the NFL Hall of Fame!

I cooked what remained of the T-bone steak and sat sullenly eating it. I felt completely deflated, like a Christmas tree with all of its tinsel blown off. How did that cat get in the washer without making a sound and without me seeing her? Maybe "Spitinella" was Canadian for "Houdini." I noted that the lid had a rubber edging on it. That would have muffled a lot of the noise. I poked the edge of the lid with my finger. To my surprise, it opened downward quite easily. But it came to rest askew on the washer, making a quarter-moon opening. I would have seen that! Then I got an idea. I replaced the lid and snatched a cat off of the kitchen table that was sniffing around my empty plate. I held the cat even with the top of the wringer, and let it drop onto the lid. The cat went right through as the lid swung downward, completing a full somersault turn. The lid came to rest in its closed position with the cat inside. Case solved!

I had one more problem to think about. Spitinella was probably dead or dying, pinioned on some spruce tree back in the gully. If Muriel found out I was responsible for harming her favorite cat, I would face a fate far worse than death. She'd skin me alive and use my hide to line her kitty litter box. If I assembled the best liars on the planet to write myself an alibi, she'd see right through it. That's just the way she was. So, I had to get out of there. I cleaned up my mess, took the cat out of the washing machine, and hit the road.

I made myself scarce for a couple of days. But when I didn't see the lightning strike or hear the thunder roll, I became a little curious. I stopped by for a visit, trying to be nonchalant and ready to bolt and run at the same time. But I was surprised at how normal everything seemed to be. If there was any question about a missing cat, nobody was coming to me with them. Then I saw why.

Up on top of the bookcase,
Looking no worse for the wear
Sat Spitinella, or her ghost,
With a regal sort of air.
She smiled at me with an evil grin,
And licked her furry lips.

Spitnella And The T-Bone

Then she purred the tune to "The Cat Came Back,"
And my mind began to rip!
A cold sweat ran right down my back,
And my hair began to rise,
In whispered words she hissed at me,
"I still got eight more lives.
I'll come for you in the dead of night,
Your soul I'm gonna take,
Unless you come back one more time
And bring me another steak!"

CHAPTER 12
THE BURLINGTON NORTHERN

In my vault there really is a lot about trains. The bigger stories are kept in neat piles and I look into them quite often. But I also find little fragments here and there that can no longer tell a full story and I tried to lay them out to get some kind of timeline when all these little bits and pieces happened. I hope we'll get to some of those because there really are some good stories. I've said it before, how I would love to clean it up a little, the vault is quite a mess, but I can't. Also, I can't stop things from fading away. It's part of growing older, the neurons stop talking to each other till you have no idea what they are trying to say. That's why you my reader need to start writing things down. For example; to my left hanging on the wall is a clock that has been faithfully ticking away for over one hundred years now. It belonged to my great grandmother. She was always referred to as, "little gramma Sayre" because, well, she was little. There is a picture inside the clock of me as a toddler sitting on her lap. I look like some gargantuan child. But it wasn't me being big, it was her being small. Anyway, there was a really good story about grandma; when she was six years old, they moved into the frontier town of Minneapolis. At the time Indians still inhabited an island out in the middle of the Mississippi River, the island is still there today. Over a span of only two days the number of Indians doubled and there was a lot of dancing and whooping it up going on out there on the island. The settlers were afraid this might be a precursor to an Indian uprising. Three days later the white people found out what the Indians had known for days; the defeat of General George Armstrong Custer at the Battle of the Little Bighorn.

Another good story came from my grandfather, her son, about something he saw when he was just a little boy. He was down at the railroad station; I think he said he was around ten years old. He saw stacks of flattened Buffalo hides piled one on top of another to a height of ten feet, and the stacks of hides went down the loading dock as far as he could see. I'm thinking of the stories they could have told if they had only thought to write them down. So, keep a journal. Some day you might have a book of you!

So given my interest in trains it should come as no surprise that I ended up working on the railroad. My brother Garron started working for the Burlington Northern on March 1, 1970. If you cared to look it up you would find that is the very day that the former SP&S, the Great Northern and the Burlington Route merged to become the Burlington Northern Railroad. Four months later I hired on as well. We worked on different teams but we were doing the same work, installing centralized traffic control, or CTC, up the Columbia River Gorge. It did just what its name suggests, gave them control of trains over hundreds of miles of track from a single location.

My first day at work I was riding on a small motor car with a foreman named Zurl Potts. He told me to keep an eye out for a train that might be coming up behind us! Was he kidding? We had put the motor car on the rails, just the two of us. So, maybe he was on the level. These motor cars had two cycle engines with a spark advance lever. If you wanted to go forward, you simply moved the spark advance forward, and using your hand, spin the wheel on the side of the engine to start it and you would go forward. If you wanted to go backwards you would stop the engine, move the spark lever and start the engine in reverse, simple as that.

Both aforementioned crews were hired for the purpose of installing the CTC, or centralized traffic control, and it was going to require a lot of climbing. They issued all the essential climbing gear, which consisted of climbing spurs that strapped onto your boots and around your leg, a heavy tool belt and a scare strap. Both ends of the scare strap hung from a "D" ring on the left side of your tool belt. When you got to the pole you would unhook one end of the scare strap, loop it around the pole, then hook it into the "D" ring on your right side. My foreman's name was Gordon, and he offered up a short tutorial on how to climb polls. He said there was only two things you needed to know: keep your spurs sharp, and always, always lean out away from the pole.

When you first learn to climb you desperately want to cling to the pole with your arms, but you can't do that because it changes the angle of your spurs to the pole you're climbing, and you'll burn the pole. You don't want to do that!

I took to climbing like a duck takes to water; in just a short period of time I was among the best climbers on both crews. It wasn't long before I became the "go to" guy when we came across a pole that was leaning, or a really tall pole or sometimes a rotten one. They'd say "oh, here's a George pole." I didn't mind it. I developed a trick that nobody could copy. Most of the time the tracks are on fill which puts the poles about five feet down from the level of the tracks. Instead of walking downhill to the pole I would simply jump across that distance and land half way up on the pole, thus saving time and energy. I only know of one guy who tried that; it didn't turn out too good for him.

In the three years that I worked for the BN Railroad we had extended the CTC over 100 miles up the tracks from Vancouver, WA all the way up to a little town called Wishram. The CTC required two additional wires to be pulled in, and we referred to these as code wires. They were installed on the North End of the bottom cross arm, so whatever was on the North End had to be moved because they wanted it uniform all the way through the system.

We were always pulling line wire off of spools, all six of us pulling one behind the other. We pulled wire along the track, then up over the bluffs and then back down to the tracks again. After we had pulled out about a mile of wire, it was time to start climbing poles. Day after day the same thing. The only time we got a break from line wire is when we were sent somewhere to install a new crossing signal. One problem we ran into was poison oak; it grows everywhere in the Columbia River Gorge, and there were times when the wire had to be pulled right through the middle of it. When that happened, we would pull up a big pile of slack in the wire and then take it around the poison oak and when we got around it, we would fling the wire up in the air and pull it tight over the patch of poison oak. But it wasn't long before I came to realize that I was immune to the effect of poison oak. It turns out it didn't bother me a bit; I could walk bare chested right through the middle clear up to my armpits in poison oak and it wouldn't bother me at all, so I became very useful.

When I started working for the Railroad, our outfit cars were parked on a siding in a place called Skamania. They consisted of two box cars for tools and supplies, one car we used as a dining hall/kitchen, and a fourth one had bunk beds from end to end in it, with an old oil heater in the middle. I stayed there for six months until I got married, and I remember one incident we had with the heater. We weren't there at the time, but the dang thing blew up leaving the coach filled with two inches of soot from end to end. It was quite a job cleaning it up, and I was glad no one was there when it blew. For some time, I had noticed the smoke coming out of the stove didn't look right. It was black and stringy looking.

The Vault

There were a number of tunnels that the tracks went through and most of them were short. We could just run the line wire up over the top on the hill above the tunnel. But there was one tunnel that was a mile long, and we had to dig a ditch and bury a cable all way through. The tunnel curved a little and you didn't have to get very far in before you couldn't see either portal, and if the lights ever went out you would be in trouble. The supervisors had put a slow order on the tunnel, which meant trains would have to reduce their speed to ten or fifteen miles an hour through the tunnel. Both crews were working the site, so that put it at twelve to fourteen men in the tunnel. Well, that was a good idea except the first train in the tunnel came through at speed, that's sixty miles an hour, and it just scared the crap out of all of us. From then on, we worked in accordance with the lineup of trains which was given out each morning. That and a book called the time table told how soon a train could be expected at our mile post. This gave us time to clear the tunnel before the train arrived. One concern of working in close proximity to a moving train is broken loading straps. These straps are found mostly on flatbed cars, and they usually hold bunks of lumber or any other crated goods. These steel straps become dangerous if one end breaks loose for any reason; you can have a twenty-five-foot-long strap of metal bouncing along the side of a train. We were warned of men having serious lacerations, and even arms and legs torn off by these straps.

Ken stood beside the motor car, fumbling in his pocket for the line-up copied that morning. The 6-man signal crew, which included my brother Garron, had disembarked the motor car for the second time in as many minutes. They had heard a train whistle, so they had stopped, turned off the engine, and stood there beside the railroad tracks, listening. They were right next to Beacon Rock out of Skamania, Washington. The men decided that the whistle was coming from the Union Pacific across the river on the Oregon side. The sound was bouncing off Beacon Rock, a phenomenon well known by the men of the BN Railroad. The rock rose 848 feet above the majestic Columbia River, making it the world's second largest monolith, next to the Rock of Gibraltar. They reseated themselves in the open cab, started the motor, and headed down the rails, when they heard it again, louder. They stopped again, and this time the lead man consulted the line-up, which showed this section of track to be clear for at least two hours. It had to be the Union Pacific. They had just gotten underway for the third time, when around the corner came a west-bound freight train.

We heard all the details back in camp for weeks to come. I will give you my brother's account of this catastrophe, because he used his head and got the best view. Having anything impeding rail traffic was to a railroad worker the number one taboo. There were all kinds of safety precautions to prevent this sort of thing, yet here they were, a large crew-sized motor car pulling a cart full of heavy pins and insulators was about to have a head-on collision. Somebody said the headlight on that lead engine looked like it was fourteen feet across. The whole crew jumped and ran for their lives. The motor car and everything on it was going to be destroyed and sent flying like shrapnel for hundreds of feet in every direction. If the train itself was derailed, the path of destruction would have been 200 feet wide and 1,000 feet long. The terrified men were running in every direction. One man tore himself up trying to run through a barbed wire fence. But as I said earlier, Garron used his head. He ran uphill, toward the train. When he got to what he thought was a safe distance, he turned around to watch. You don't see this sort of thing every day. He said when the cowcatcher on the front of the engine hit the cart, it was like a case of dynamite being set off. Pins and insulators erupted with incredible force. He saw the train crew hit the deck as the windows broke, and the front of the engine was peppered with flying debris. The train cut through the motor car like it was made of aluminum foil and deposited pieces of it for hundreds of feet down the track. Except for cuts and scratches, and dirty underwear, no one was seriously hurt. The only thing identifiable in the debris field was one wheel from the motor car.

It turns out that it was the fault of the man with the most seniority in the former SP&S Railroad, Zurl Potts. He had made a mistake copying that morning's line-up. His punishment was 1 month off without pay. Seems a small price for what could have gotten people killed.

The Burlington Northern

Me and my little "five foot two and eyes of blue" were married on February 5, 1971. We rented a small two-bedroom house in the town of North Bonneville; it was only a stone's throw from the end of the Bonneville Dam. Some years later the whole town of North Bonneville was entirely removed to make room for a second powerhouse on the Bonneville Dam. I think when they first built the dam, they didn't know what they would do with all the electricity it could generate, so they only put in the one powerhouse.

Our first daughter was born when we were living there, and I was completely unprepared for what that little bundle was going to do to me. I had been around babies, lots of them, and my idea was, they were a short tube with a loud noise on one end and a complete lack of control on the other. But when I held her for the first time and looked into those big round eyes, something happened deep down inside of me; I can't put a name to it. She was a little human being, perfect all the way down to her little toes. We made her and she was wonderful. What was the odds of that happening on your first try? I found out right away that I didn't have to brag about how perfect she was because people did it for me. Everywhere we went, getting groceries, the drug store, or just going for a walk, and especially at church, complete strangers would come up and just go gaga all over her. It was like walking around with a box full of puppies. Another thing I would like to add is our landlady dropped our rent, from $60.00 per month to $50.00. That don't happen anymore.

The Vault

I am an old man now and I have seen this happen time and time again, with my children and grandchildren and young couples everywhere. When they first get married it's all lovey dovey, and that's good. But when they have their first child something changes in them; I've seen it over and over again, it's a godly sort of thing that changes little girls and boys into loving parents; it's beautiful. One more thought; your parents raised you, but your kids will finish the job.

One day I was exploring our neighborhood on the south side of town closest to the Bonneville Dam. It was mostly wooded with small houses plopped down here and there. I got to the end of this one road, and found there were three structures nestled in among the trees, one on my right, another straight ahead and a singlewide mobile to my left. It was then that I noticed something of concern; the smoke coming out of the chimney of the mobile home didn't look right, it was jet black and stringy. It looked just like the smoke that was coming out of the heater in our old outfit car just before it blew up. I went over, knocked on the door and asked in a loud voice "is there anybody in here?" I heard a feeble voice calling out for help! I opened the door and saw the house was full of heavy smoke down to within three feet of the floor. I could see through the smoke-filled room a couch, and a frail old woman who apparently was unable to get up. I ran over and gently picked her up, carried her outside and carefully sat her in a lawn chair. Then I went back into the house and turned the valve off on the back of the oil stove, and used her phone to call the fire department. I found a blanket on the end of the couch and took it out and wrapped it around her. She seemed to be pretty rattled. I talked with her and told her help was on the way. I don't remember much more of this incident but I was glad to see the paramedics and the fire trucks arrive. The man who was the North Bonneville Police Department also showed up and he took a statement from me. He must have considered me a first-rate citizen because he gave me a pass on a couple of things that I should have gotten a ticket for, like the time I came through town doing twice the legal speed limit. He got me on radar, lights came on and he started to pull out, but when he saw it was me, he turned the lights off and moved back into his parking spot. Another time I was burning insulation off of wire so I could sell the copper. It was at night and I heard a knock on my door. When I open the door there was our local constable, and he informed me that the entire town was socked in with the black smoke I was making. He asked if I could change my brand of firewood; he knew what I was doing. Well, I of course agreed to do just that, and that was the end of it. He could have given me a pretty big ticket for that one.

As we continued installing CTC up the Columbia River, the outfit cars needed to be moved a third time. They were at Skamania first, then North Bonneville, and that was handy for me. Now the cars were moved to a siding in a little town called Lyle. So, we decided to move up river to Bingen, just across from Hood River.

The Vault

In my third and final year on the railroad, we were pulling in line wire upriver from The Dalles Dam. I came to discover that we were in an area that had been occupied for thousands of years by the Native Americans. We were pulling in line wire through the great fishing grounds of Celilo Falls. If you use google earth, find the Dalles Dam and follow along up river till you find Horsethief Lake; it's on the Washington side. That is the site of Wakemap Mound. "Wakemap" is an anglicized word for "old Woman," and was pronounced "Wok'um'up." This mound, or Tel, is the longest continuously occupied site in the Americas; they figure around 13,000 years. The Dalles Dam was going to flood all of this site, so in the early '50s archaeologists did a major dig in this area. But for over fifty years, private citizens had scoured this land looking for Indian artifacts. If you still have your Google Maps open, take a look at the land just south of Horsethief Lake and you'll see little round indentations which marked the spot of private excavations. I even read someplace that just days before the flooding of The Dalles Dam there was somebody down in there with a Caterpillar scraping the ground up looking for relics. I remember one day we broke for lunch right by the river. They must have opened the floodgates on the dam and allowed a bunch of water to go out, because in just the twenty minutes we sat there eating, a mudflat appeared. The six of us walked out on the mudflat and we all picked up a handful of arrowheads in just a matter of minutes.

There is something I have not spoken of and that is drugs and alcohol. It was a big problem on the railroad. Almost everyone used alcohol, some to excess. Among the druggies there were two groups; the downers like heroin, and the uppers like "speed." I was an assistant foreman by this time, so I went with speed because it got things done. I remember a lot of days where we would go out to our assigned location, and with most everybody speeding, we would get the job done by the end of the morning. Then we would sneak off someplace, take the rest of the day off and smoke pot. This was a growing problem for me. I remember one day we were setting a signal foundation using our high rail boom truck. The high rail, if you don't know, has wheels that can be lowered down onto the railroad tracks so you can go by rail to any place the work required. We broke for lunch, and when everybody was about done someone lit up a joint and was passing it around. I normally wouldn't have taken it because we had a truck on the rails! But I was getting a little wired from the speed, so I took one puff of the joint, and I got smashed! I was tripping one minute and freaking out the next. I was too stoned to make the compilation for when the next train was due at our location. I mean it was complicated. The daily line-up would read something like "extra 185 out of MX at 2:25 p.m.," then you use the time table to configure when the train would be at your milepost. MX was Vancouver, or milepost 1. We were at milepost seventy-nine???? Then if that wasn't bad enough my boss showed up and wanted to talk! Well, all I could do was listen. If I tried to say anything I would have given myself away for sure. Later I found out he was apologizing for sending me out with the crew so much. So being quiet was probably the right move. But this was not working. I couldn't keep living like this.

Then one day I took my stupidity to a new level. One of the guys on my gang had received permission to take off half a day for personal reasons. I found out that he was going to a town up north to buy some mescaline, a synthesized hallucinogenic that originally came from the peyote cactus. I threw down my shovel and said; "well, I'm going too," and off I went. As a result, I was also off work, without pay, pending an investigation. With two kids and a wife this was a big deal. On the railroad they didn't just fire you when you screwed up, they had to have an investigation first.

The next morning, I stood at the end of our sidewalk looking up and down the street. I noticed the houses, the trees, the cars, everything looked so clear and I didn't know why. But as I stood there thinking, it dawned on me that I was straight; straight as in not stoned. Well, I thought, this hadn't happened for a while. I assure you it was not intentional. I just happened to be out of drugs at the time. No weed, no speed, no pills, no big deal. I had just started mainlining amphetamines and that was a big deal. As a matter of fact, it was scaring the hell out of me – needles! Taking this personal inventory out at the end of our sidewalk was the perfect time for God to show up, and He did. A picture came into my mind of myself standing, not on the sidewalk, but on the edge of a cliff. I took it to mean a bad thing.

Looking back over the last year I could see where I had turned off the path. I could not live the Christian life no matter how hard I tried. So, at some point in time, I thought it better to consider myself to be non-Christian rather than be a Constant embarrassment to Christ. I was writing songs as far back as I can remember and they reflected this feeling of frustration as seen in the following song;

> ***"Father please help me, tell me what to do, once more I have gone the wrong way. All that I do seems to be the wrong thing and I long for the peace that your perfect will brings…"***

So, I went to see the preacher. We talked. He asked some questions to see if I understood the plan of salvation, which I did. Then of all things he sent me to visit his son, whom I had never met. He was recuperating in the hospital from some minor surgery. I had his name, Phil, and his room number, but I didn't know why I should be seeing this guy. I remember thinking on the way to the hospital that I was the one looking for a little help here, so why am I going to see this guy? Well, it was from God without question. Phil hit the mark as if he had been in preparation for this moment his entire life. We talked for a long time and he gave me the following three verses;

Isaiah 40:30-31 "Even the youths shall faint and be weary, and the young men shall utterly fall;" well that, I felt, was a perfect description of my life. "But they that wait upon the Lord shall renew their strength; they shall mount up with wings as eagles, they shall run and not be weary; and they shall walk and not faint." I felt like a car with a flat tire being lifted up off the pavement with a bumper jack. I felt hope. The "run and not be weary" I understood to be the big battle that you buck yourself up to fight; you are ready for this. But the "walk and not faint," that is what got me every time, the day to day, same old - same old living that catches you off your guard. When the days are hot, the work is hard, and the weeks are long, that is when the true test of "living by faith" begins.

Romans 14:22 "Happy is he who does not condemn himself in what he approves." Oh, this was simple housekeeping; there was no joy to this, only practical advice. If you allow junk in, you'll get junk out.

Philippians 3:13-14 "But one thing I do, forgetting those things which are behind and reaching forward to those things which are ahead, I press toward the goal for the prize of the upward call of God in Christ Jesus." The raw power of the word of God, to change lives, hit me like a ton of bricks. The devil had this cassette tape of all the rotten things committed by Georgie Porgie, and every time I tried to live for Christ, he would at some point pop that baby in and play it to my perpetual mortification. But when I read the words; "forgetting those things which are behind "I was set free by the power of God's word. I saw my attachment to those many failings being stretched and stretched like some infinite pull of taffy, until at last it broke in two, with the ends flying off into eternity. The change was like black and white, like being hit by holy lightning. I was a new creation.

At the investigation everyone was completely blown away. I was honest, and I was humble before God and man. They saw a changed person; no matter what I had done in the past, they could find no guile in me whatsoever. I got my job back and I started "working as unto the Lord." In the past I missed so many days that I don't think I ever drew a full pay check, and I was constantly late for work. Now I was not only on time, but I got there before everybody, unlocked the doors and turned on the lights. I had such a zeal for God and it splashed out over everything I did. Victories and new insights came on a daily basis.

Between the two signal gangs there were about fourteen men, and at the start of each day we would all be at the office to get the daily lineup of trains and find out what the day's project would be. One morning the foreman of the other crew, Zerl, had found a New Testament somewhere, and in front of all the men he presented it to me as a joke. Every eye was on me, there was sure to be a big laugh in this. But God gave me a spirit of grace to accept that New Testament as if it were a priceless work of art. I thanked him profusely for the little testament and embraced it with love. It became sort of an embarrassment for everyone in the room, like they were going to make sport of something that became holy right in front of their eyes. I carried it with me from then on. I remember one rainy day we were tying in line wire, and as I was walking to the next pole, I pulled the testament out of my pocket. As I opened it the sun broke thru the clouds and shone on the page. I read till I got to the next pole, put the testament back in my pocket, the sun went out and I climbed the next pole. It made me feel like God himself was right there with me. One day we were installing a crossing signal when one of the guys, a particular vile individual called out "Hey George, quote us some of your scripture." Without hesitation, and as big of a surprise to me as to anyone, I shot back with "Give not that which is holy unto the dogs, neither cast your pearls before the swine..." Matt. 7:6. I had never memorized that, but there it was. The guy who had asked said; "Hey, I think I've been insulted."

On the home front I had to find something to fill all the time I had involved in doing drugs, so I started gardening. Then I showed up at church every time the doors where open. Christian coffee houses were a big thing back then, so the pastor's son, Mark, and I started a coffee house. It seemed then that nothing was too difficult; God's blessing was on everything I put my hand to.

I had mentioned earlier that I was getting to work early each day. What I didn't say is I left home in time to take a detour off the main road that ran up the Columbia River Gorge. There was this narrow road that wound its way up over the high bluffs of the gorge. I had found an overlook that was just gorgeous. I would park my car and walk over to the edge of the bluff; with the sun rising at my left, I would pray in the new day.

Our Pastor, whom we became very fond of, encouraged me to memorize a scripture, personalize it, and then use Gods own words to pray back to him. So, I started with Psalm 139 in the New Living Bible. "Oh Lord, you have examined my heart and know everything about me..." what a wonderful scripture. After I had memorized it, I started to think what it meant to me personally. I remember the day when I was ready to meet with God using His own words. I stood there on the bluff, with a glorious sunrise turning the whole length of the Columba River valley to gold. I raised my hands and I started to pray Psalm 139, "Oh daddy, you know my heart completely, you know my posture, when far away you know my thoughts. You set the path before me and tell me when to rest. You always know where I am and what I'm going to say even before I say it. This is too glorious, too wonderful to believe! ... I can never be lost to your spirit! I can never get away from you! If I go up to heaven, you are there; if I go down to the place of the dead, you are there. If I ride the morning winds to the farthest oceans, even there your hand will guide me; your strength will support me..."

I really don't remember the exact words I prayed. But I do remember this was as far as I was able to go through that Psalm. It became my "Mount of transfiguration," the closest I would ever get to God. I felt His presence so close,

His power so great, His holiness so awesome, I could not continue. I had to ask Him to stop His blessing. It was not exactly fear. I felt like I would blow apart. The thought somehow came to me in that very moment of time, that the people who came looking for me would find big chunks of me lying all over the ground. There is nothing I have longed for in my entire life more than to be this close to God. If I had known this would become my high-water mark, I would have let her blow. Our lives moved on to different places and different times. I have been back to that mountain a few times. I tried to pray as I did those years ago, but to no avail.

So, I have to ask, why was I, a young upstart of a C-minus Christian, allowed such an audience with God? And why has it never happened again? I'll tell you; I haven't got a clue except maybe we really can't live on mountain tops. When Moses came down from Mount Sinai, his face shone so he had to be veiled. One thing I do know; it's not helpful to ask why, or to consider it a fall from God's grace. I think it was a gift, one that came with a new kind of hunger for God, like a child who longs to crawl into his daddy's lap. "As the deer pants for water, so pants my soul for you, O God." [Ps. 42]

Is God still in the mountain? Yes. But I think we find him more often in the valley, when our hearts are broken. In loss, in sorrow, in failure, we find God right where we left him. David said; "A broken and contrite heart, O God, you will not despise." [Ps. 51:17]. So, is it some hidden sin that costs us the mountain? I think so. But before you go embrace asceticism remember, we know about sin like a fish knows he's wet. It is our environment, this fallen world.

As often as I pass through the Columba River Gorge, I think of those years I worked there surrounded by such beauty. In a span of three years, I became a first-rate lineman, I got married, my two daughters were born, and I was delivered from a lifetime of self regrets. Oh, and another thing, I never used drugs again. You never know when you're living through the good old days, until they're gone.

My last day at the Burlington northern railroad only lasted about five minutes. My foreman, Gordon, had moved on and was replaced by a man named Art who was a lineman in his fifties. The first thing I knew of him, he was having a midlife crisis. He left his wife and home and moved in with an eighteen-year-old girl whose house just happened to be about ten feet from our back door. At some point he came to his senses and moved back in with his wife. He did not like me; I was a witness to all of his foolishness with the eighteen-year-old.

My wife and I were already thinking about moving back to Vancouver. So, when I got to work one morning Art started griping at me for something I had nothing to do with. So, I walked right past him into the tool room and motioned for Art to follow. I almost laughed when I saw the look on his face, like he was going to get his ass handed to him. I thought, not a bad idea, but instead I pulled my tool bag off the shelf, opened it and dumped it all out right at his feet. I reached down and got my lineman pliers, and looked Art right in the face and said, "these are the tools that were checked out to me. I'm going on vacation. If I don't come back, you'll know I quit."

I drove back to Bingen, picked up Millie and the kids, and a pickup load of our stuff, and drove the eighty miles to Vancouver. I rented a duplex, unloaded the truck, drove over to Portland to the local Boilermaker union and hired on as a welder/fitter for FMC at Swan Island dry dock, all in one day. I had a lot more energy in those days.

CHAPTER 13
A TINY TOWN ON A HUGE PRAIRIE

Miller Memorial Bible Institute moved to the small town of Pambrun, Saskatchewan at the start of World War II. We heard about the school from a man named Johnny Macknee, who came to the small church we were going to when I was still working on the railroad. It sounded very interesting, so about three years later we sold the mobile home we were living in and moved to Pambrun.

Millie, myself and our two daughters came from the Evergreen State of Washington where they had trees, rivers, mountains, and lakes, so life on the prairie was a real adjustment for us. We really missed the trees. You could look for miles in any direction and there wouldn't be a single tree, except for those planted around our little town for a windbreak to stop the snow from drifting. I think there were five rows of trees, and we would walk down the middle of the windbreak without looking to the left or the right and feel like we were "back in God's country." The first song I wrote about our new location conjured up words like "vapid icy tomb." The locals were not impressed. But, our feelings about the prairies began to soften a little. I remember the first big storm to move into our location. There was this huge, dark bank of clouds marching across the prairies. It made you think of an approaching army. Hoarfrost in the winter would cling to every tree branch and looked like coins all stacked up on edge. When the temperatures were really low you could see these tiny ice crystals floating around in the air reflecting the sunshine, it was mesmerizing. There was a small window in my study that looked out onto this frozen landscape. Our little house was right on the edge of town and we could see the grain elevators across the railroad tracks that marked our little town from miles away. I could also see our fuel tank with a gauge displaying our dwindling supply of stove oil. For some reason our fuel tank was a favorite hangout for the local sparrows. They were very entertaining, so much so that I wrote the following poem.

SPARROWS

In every climate country, in every hemisphere
We find a feathered creature who stays around all year.
He seems to be God's answer to man's oft toil and strain,
For these tiny common sparrows were made to entertain.
He fluffs his drab brown feathers to almost twice their size
And shouts to all humanity the way to thermalize.
Such chubby little sparrows their feathers never neat,

***Oft times I sit and wonder about their little feet.
How do they keep from freezing; I think I'll never know,
Especially when the mercury drops to forty-plus below.
But through my winter window all done in icy lace
I watch these crazy acrobats possessing little grace.
They roll and fight and tumble amidst the frozen air.
How do they ever stay aloft? It's plain, they just don't care.
But I'm thankful God has sent them to flutter here and there
To brighten up the commonplace and lighten loads of care.***

I liked Canadians, still do. They have a wonderful sense of humor. But they had a different way of talking that you had to get used to. The word "eh" I found out, could be used as a question mark, an exclamation mark, or a statement. It was a handy piece of verbiage and I kind of miss it. I wish we had something like it down here in Montana, eh. There were two universal topics of conversation among the locals, wheat and hockey. I think if they got together and couldn't discuss either one, they would probably just sit there with their hands folded in their lap and say nothing at all.

On February 5, 1977 we celebrated our sixth wedding anniversary. Up till then we had always made a big deal out of our anniversary dates. But money was a little short that year so our celebration consisted of a drive to the next town,

Vanguard, where we purchased a candy bar which we split between the two of us. Hooray!

In the winter of 1977-1978, Star Wars was playing at the theater in Swift Current. We weren't sure but we guessed it was probably a taboo for us to sneak off to see a movie, but I'm sure glad we did. We were transported light years away from Pambrun Saskatchewan in a way that was just positively transforming. What a great movie! I don't think we've had a movie that affected us as much as that one did, well until "JAWS," came along.

Our son was born on December 10, 1977 right in the middle of midterm finals. Millie had an appointment on that date, and because there had been blizzard warnings for the last two weeks in a row the doctor made the decision to induce labor. I was given a cap and gown, and ushered right into the delivery room and got to see the whole thing for the first time in my life. I had two girls, and in the US the custom was for you to be in the smoke-filled waiting room with all the other nervous fathers. I was really hoping for a boy. When he was born, I could see that there was a good chance it was a boy, but I knew they still had to snip some things off, so I waited until the proclamation came. It's a boy! And then they did the dumbest thing ever. They took that brand new tiny, helpless baby, and put him right into my clumsy hands. Didn't they know I was sure to drop him? It was almost shocking and it had a profound effect on me. It rattled around in my head for years until it finally popped out in a song. I'll give you just a part of it, maybe you can see for yourself how it affected me. How could God have done such a thing?

> *The mighty God, the creator, the ruler of this world, became a baby, to set men free, just a tiny baby, you could hold him in your hands, just a tiny baby in Bethlehem.*

Of the many friends we made at Bible school there were none better than Jack and Bea Retzer. They came to school with their two kids and lived in a triplex right next to our little house on the prairie. We are still close friends and keep in touch. Jack came to Pambrun to get theological training, but he showed up at school with a pastor's heart. I've only known a few men who had the ability to show real compassion, be able to listen well and give good advice, and Jack was one of those. Then he always ended with a prayer that seemed to make everything better. He was very popular with the young students and is still using his gift as I write this. Jack and Bea have known each other since they were in the third grade, and are about to celebrate their 65th wedding anniversary.

I would also like to tell you about Edwin Murphy. He was not a great student but he will, I believe, be one of those rare individuals who will hear the sought-after words; "well done thou good and faithful servant." Edwin could not communicate with the written word. He could not create a proper sentence, and I don't think he passed very many tests in the three years he was at bible school. But he faithfully returned for all three years in spite of that. Edwin loved the Lord, and I cannot overstate his faithfulness. He did more with the little ability he had than most of the people I know, myself included.

Edwin started in a ministry that has lasted over forty-three years and he's still going. Each year he started in the spring working at a sheep ranch, where I am guessing he made most of his money for the year. Then he spent the summers working at Big Sky Bible Camp located in Big Fork, Montana. When kids camp was over, he worked in a number of nursing homes around Western Montana telling Bible stories using flannel graphs. I also heard that he worked in child evangelism and another ministry that helped kids in rural communities learn about the bible. When we get to heaven, I think I'll be shining Edwin's shoes.

Miller was a conservative school, and at the end of a three-year course they handed out a diploma. I never aspired to the notion of becoming a pastor. I guess I'm just not cut from that kind of cloth. But the school was very missionary minded and I thought that might be something I could do. So, after graduation I signed up with Northern Canada Evangelical Mission headquartered in Lac La Biche, Alberta. They were offering a four-month missionary training course, which sounded to me like a good place to start.

CHAPTER 14
Northern Canada Evangelical Mission

We spent one week in Lac La Biche for orientation and cultural training camp. Working with Indians is different. Trying to get my mind around how they thought about things was something I don't think I was very successful at. We did find out that we would be working with mostly Cree and Metis Indians. The Cree Indians we were told were very straightforward. If they didn't like you, they would come right to your face and tell you so. The Metis Indians on the other hand would treat you like their best friend. If there was anything they didn't like about you, they never let on until they came to a certain point, then it would all come flying out. I found this to be very accurate. I don't know if things are still like this today, but in 1980 I had a neighbor, a very good friend, Norman, who just blew up all over me because I called his cat "scrawny." There was alcohol involved.

During the training camp we had a very intense discussion one day about working in a geographical area that had no Christian influences, no churches, no Christian history of any kind. We were told that evil was not hindered in these areas. The instructor went on to give examples which literally made the hair stand up on the back of my neck. We were told of a young couple working on language study in a certain village who were constantly ill. They tried and tried to find a cure for whatever was ailing them, to no avail. It was then that their overseer asked them if they had received any artwork or other handmade items from the natives. Well, they answered in the affirmative, showing him a small wall hanging they had received several weeks earlier. The overseer took the piece of carved wood outside and burned it. Almost right away their illness started to leave them. He told us they could put medicine on a dog and it would follow the missionaries everywhere they went. The dog would stay exactly the same distance away; if they stopped the dog stopped, if they went into their house the dog would sit outside their house and watch. This man who was telling us all this I would consider to be a very sensible, conservative individual. He told us he was in language study with a couple one summer day; it was a warm day so the door was standing open. He said a cat came in through the door and stood in the middle of the living room and spoke to them in English. As many times as I have told this story someone will always ask "what did the cat say?" Well, he never told us. I don't think he wanted to draw our attention to the black arts, but only the existence of them.

When our week of orientation was done, we headed east through Saskatchewan to a town called Meadow Lake. NCEM had a radio station there and we made some recordings of our music to be used on the air. There was a shortage of western-style Christian music at the time. The next day we headed north where we would spend most of the summer.

Two-hundred miles of gravel road on a very hot day left us covered with dust as we arrived in Ile-a-la-Crosse. We found our "house," which was also covered in dust. It was small, maybe twelve feet wide by fifteen feet long, and at some point, a lean-to had been added, increasing the size of the house by a third. The only problem was the lean-to had pulled away from the house leaving a four-to-five-inch gap all around. It was like a come on in to anything rat-sized or smaller. The house smelled of sour wine and stale beer, and had not been lived in for a long time. However, there was a refrigerator and one bare light bulb, courtesy of an extension cord stretched over from the house next door. There was a table that had to lean against the wall or it would fall over, and four chairs. There was no running water, and we cooked on a camp stove that we brought with us. The house was filthy and had to be washed before we could sleep, and the only water available that we knew of was down next to the lake. Somebody gave us a clean plastic garbage can with which we could haul water back to the house from the lake. There were two cotton mats brought over from the detox center in town, but the floor had to be washed where we would lay the mats down. We were getting pretty tired. However, we had to clean ourselves up first and there was no other place to do it but down at the lake. So, we put on some swimsuits, and with an audience of about twenty or thirty little kids we proceeded to wash ourselves up in the lake. An extra big wave came along and knocked Millie over, and she lost our bar of soap. From then on, we started using ivory soap because it floated.

With the house somewhat clean, Millie made up our bed on the floor using the cotton mats and we crawled in. Boy we were tired. But those cotton mats were terrible; they felt like they were stuffed with dead cats. I was trying to get to sleep when Millie suddenly sat bolt upright in bed and told God in no uncertain terms that she could not do this. She wanted a brand new, clean, four-inch-thick, double-wide foam mattress. Then she cried herself to sleep.

The next morning there was a knock at the door and Millie went to see who it was. There standing before her was a native man carrying a big bundle which he pushed into her arms, as he informed her that "Ralph" told him to give this to her. It turned out to be the brand-new four-inch, double-wide foam rubber mattress Millie had asked for. Millie turned back to the door to ask who Ralph was, but there was no one there – the man had disappeared. So, two observations here; prayer changes things, we knew that, and somewhere among the starry hosts there's an Angel named Ralph. Thank you, Ralph, that was very kind of you!

We had our eighteen-month-old son Daniel with us, but we had to leave our two girls with friends and that was really hard. When we arrived at Ile-a-la-Crosse Millie was already missing the girls, and she started crying right away. I waited until the next morning before I started to cry. But Daniel was a real icebreaker with the natives. It turns out that they are very fond of the babies, but once their kids get grown up a little, they're kind of on their own. It was common when inquiring about somebody's kids as to their whereabouts to hear that they were "somewhere in the village." There were lots of aunts and uncles to help keep an eye on them. We started a weekly Bible club for the kids. There was music, Bible stories, and a huge bowl of popcorn, which they inhaled in about five minutes. We did not have to advertise or go looking for kids; the popcorn did the trick because the kids would spread the news all on their own. I think we had half the kids in the village show up, which was all we could handle.

The village dance hall was only about 200 feet away from our little house. There was no bathroom or outhouse for the dance hall, so they just used our outhouse which was the closest one around. We found that out on the very first day. Millie had gone to use the outhouse and ran into the biggest Native American either one of us had ever seen. His name was Peter. It scared Millie half to death, and she started talking really loud so that I could hear and hopefully come to her aid. Well as it turns out Peter was the proverbial gentle giant, although slightly inebriated. I should also add here that there was behind the outhouse a growing pile of disposable diapers. I remember sharing this oddity with a Bush pilot who flew for NCEM. He told me about, not a pile, but a mountain of disposable diapers in a town sixty miles to the north called Canoe Narrows. He said when flying at altitude you could see that pile from forty miles away shining in the sun like some kind of a jewel.

I had mentioned Norman earlier. He and his wife Elisabeth had become good friends. I learned a lot from them. For one thing, the native people were not very materialistic. For example, I was talking to him one day about snowmobiles and how I hoped to have one someday. He told me that he had a brand new one. "Well, let's go have a look at it," I said, but Norman said we couldn't. When I asked him why, he said "it's out in the bush." The "bush" is how they refer to the millions of acres of timber that surrounds them. Apparently, it had run out of gas the winter before and it was still "in the bush" right where he left it. I being a white man would tend to keep a tight grip on my possessions, but the natives were different. It seems everyone owned a flat-bottom boat with a forty-horse Johnson outboard on it. When finished they would run them up on the bank and leave them untethered, with the motors still hanging in the water. In a way I suppose I admire them because I'm too materialistic. I forget all this stuff that I cling to will either be lost in life or left in death. Another thing I learned from Norman is that you never swat a mosquito. You gently swish it away from you. I wanted to smash every one that landed on me and send them all to mosquito hell. But I noticed sitting in the group of three other men that I was the only one getting bit by mosquitoes. Norman explained to me that when you swat a mosquito you leave a blood scent that draws other mosquitoes to you. Mosquitoes are a big problem, and the people in the north have had to learn how to live with them. One thing you will notice, most all of the villages are built on the shore of a lake. There is almost always a breeze blowing off the water and that's the one thing mosquitoes can't deal with, wind. They never plant any shrubbery, trees or even grass around their houses, as it gives the mosquitoes something to hold on to. Whenever the wind is not blowing, they build smudge fires all around the village, and that helps keep the mosquitoes away. I remember one day out on the edge of town I saw a very inviting path going into the bush. So, I went in and I can tell you that lasted about thirty seconds. Just like that, I had nine mosquitoes on one arm. I brushed them off, then I had nine mosquitoes on the other arm. I brushed them off, then nine mosquitoes on my face. I did about three or four rounds of that before I came running back out. Both man and beast have been driven mad by these demonic mosquitoes. They only have the short summers to feed, breed, and die. Now some years later when we were in Haiti, we found the mosquitoes down there to be a third of the size of the mosquitoes in the north, and they were very nonchalant about the feed, breed, and die thing because they had all year to get it done. You seldom got bit above your ankles because they were too lazy to fly any higher.

Norman and Elizabeth invited us to go on a picnic with them to an island out in the middle of the lake. Norman had one of the above-mentioned flat-bottom boats. We had a wonderful day with them. They brought four things to eat that day; a pan of Bannock, which is an Indian bread, a pound of lard, an onion, and a whitefish which is like a salmon. Norman cooked the fish over a fire and when it was done, he laid it out on a giant leaf from a plant that was growing nearby. They cut the Bannock into four-inch squares and slathered on a quarter inch of lard, and then a slice of the white onion on top of that. It doesn't sound very good, but it was delicious. During the time we were eating, a deer and a rabbit came walking right by us and showed absolutely no fear whatsoever. I guess they were never hunted out there on the island and they had no fear of man.

We ate a lot of fish that summer, Northern Pike mostly, because they were so easy to catch. It was like going to the store. One of us would say "do you want to have fish for dinner?" We would think about it and say "okay." So, we would grab our poles and go down to the lake. Almost always the first cast would bring in a two-to-three-foot-long Pike. We began to make it a competition to see who could pull in the biggest on the first cast.

Another day, another oddity. We had stopped by Norman and Elizabeth's house just to say hello. Well as it turns out, they were just ready to sit down and eat. We could see both of their plates were already filled with food. We apologized for the interruption and had intended to leave, but they insisted that we sit down and eat their meal. They could not be talked out of it and it was embarrassing to have them stand there and watch us eat their dinner, but we didn't know what else to do, so we ate.

We had the most amazing electrical storm one night; it was like nothing we had ever seen before. There were lightning strikes at every point of the compass nonstop. I have never seen anything like it since; it just went on and on and lit the whole world like day.

At the end of our time there at Ile-a-la-Crosse we were scheduled to go to a Bible camp called Pine Ridge for one week. I worked as a counselor in one of the cabins, and Millie worked in the kitchen and kept an eye on our son Daniel. The camp director's name was Lyle, and we had been in Bible school together. The week went by fast because we were so busy trying to keep up with all those kids. But it was Friday and the kids had gone home. Millie and I would not be leaving until the next morning. Lyle told us we should enjoy some personal time and take the small boat out onto the lake. He knew we were heading back to Vancouver, WA and wouldn't have a chance to be in such a wild remote spot for a long time. The boat was a 14-foot canoe with a square end that had a five-horse outboard motor on it. With Millie all the way in the front of the canoe I would get the motor started and then move up to the center of the canoe. This would flatten the canoe out and it would just go like the blazes. We could shoot across the lake, turn the motor off and just listen. We could hear moose slopping in the water two or three lakes over. It was magical! Then the mosquitoes would find us, I'd start the motor up and we shoot off to another end of the lake. We did the same thing over and over, and it was a great last night in the wilderness of northern Saskatchewan.

CHAPTER 15
THE TIME MACHINE

Port-au-Prince Haiti 1984

We sat in air-conditioned comfort rolling quietly over the hard packed dirt. We didn't talk. Don drove slowly between mud huts. Inside the car there was need of nothing. Outside there was need of most everything. We glided effortlessly through poverty, like we were in a time machine, observing life two hundred years in the past. We saw a woman cooking in an old aluminum pot over charcoal on the ground. Children mostly naked followed our vehicle with their dark eyes. Distended tummies and a reddish hue in their black hair gave evidence of malnutrition, so common in this poverty-stricken country. On the ground there was not a single blade of grass left uneaten by the scrawny, untethered goats and burros. A dog nearly starved to death was eating a grapefruit rind, while her half-grown pups tried to nurse. Hunger is an ever-present house guest, if not a close neighbor, so who cared about a starving dog. I went to bed hungry once, I thought, adjusting the visor to keep the sun out of my eyes. I was living out in the woods for a time, and a bear got into my camp and cleaned me out of food. Once in my whole life I was hungry because I had no food. One of the naked boys was waving at us. I thought if we were to offer him a ride, it would be to us like catching a ride on the space shuttle. Such overwhelming poverty was commonplace all over the whole country, but even worse here on the northern peninsula of the small Caribbean Island nation of Haiti.

Water for this village was collected in a cistern up in the mountains. Once a week the water was turned on and flowed to a single fountain head in the middle of the village until it ran out. I spent the better part of a week in this fishing village of Anse Rouge, where I learned to wash my hands and face, shave, and brush my teeth in a single cup of water, not necessarily in that order. Another oddity I discovered, and I could be wrong, is apparently there was only one pit toilet in the whole village. Right across the road from the hut I was staying in was a fairly large structure covered with rusted corrugated metal. The walls were all open, and I was directed to go down a path that led through the middle of this building. I could see on both sides of the path were little family units one after another; there must have been eight or ten families living under this one tin roof. On the far end was the pit toilet. So, every time nature called, trying not to disturb their privacy, I walked right down through the middle of all these people with my roll of paper in hand, (they mostly used rocks), and leave everybody a nice little stink bomb.

I had made the two-hour drive from Port-au-Prince to Anse Rouge to help a local pastor by the name of Stenio Capri with an evangelistic event that lasted about a week. My family had stayed in Port-au-Prince, and they had me in a small hut about ten by twelve feet with eight other guys. When Stenio arrived the next day, he chastised them saying "this guy is an American and they are not used to sleeping in such tight quarters with so many people." I told Stenio I didn't mind and we could make it work. But the next night they were all gone. It was just me, and the biggest scorpion I have ever seen in my life! I smashed him soundly with my sandal as he crawled up the wall of the mud hut, hoping he was an only child.

Haitians are very thrifty with water; they never waste it. Our house in Port-Au-Prince was supplied with water once a week. It filled a cistern in the ground, and from there we would pump it to a tank on the roof, where gravity fed it down through the house. There was a leak in the main line in front of our house and water bubbled up through cracks in the concrete road. In the year we lived in that house, I never saw one Haitian pass by that flow of water without doing something with it, drink it, wash their hands and face, or cool their feet. Many times, women would bathe themselves and their children, and wash their laundry, all the while vehicles would have to dodge around them. We only drank bottled water, but it didn't seem to help. I had dysentery all the time and weighed a good twenty-five pounds less than I do now. In another location, a woman's whole cottage industry relied on a leaky fire hydrant. She fashioned a plastic apron around the fire plug to funnel water into a can, which when full would be dumped into a wash tub, and from that she would do peoples laundry. If they ever fixed the leaky fire hydrant, she would be out of a job.

I think it was the third day after our arrival in Haiti that I went into Port-Au-Prince to help get food for the orphanage, and exchange U.S. dollars for Haitian gourdes. We were parked in the full sun for well over an hour right next to a huge pile of rotting garbage. You could see vapors shimmering out from the top of the pile, and at the bottom there was thick black goo oozing out and seeping along the ditch. People stepping up onto the side walk would carry this filth on their shoes, so the pavement was always wet with it. The heat and the smell were awful; I was close to passing out by the time we finally left there. We came here often, and once I noticed a young pregnant girl sitting on the side walk. The next time we came she was still there, and even more pregnant. So, I inquired about her and was told her father was a shoe shine boy, and while he was working, this is where she stayed. I thought this was about the worst place imaginable; why here? But she was always there. Then one day she was holding a new born. I watched as the baby grew month after month. Then one day I saw she was big enough to sit up by herself. For there she was, her little bare bottom sitting flat on that filthy side walk. Oh God have mercy! I thought about how we always put a clean blanket on the carpet for our babies to lay on. The next time I came to exchange my currency the baby was gone, but the girl was still in her usual place. I did not need to inquire about the baby; the hollow-eyed look on her face told all there was to tell.

Another time, we heard from some missionaries who ran a medical clinic, about a baby they were caring for that had almost one hundred and fifty bites all over it. When asked what had happened, they said the mother had no crib or anything to keep the baby up off the ground, and at night the rats would come in and feed on the baby. They could not bring the infections under control, and the baby died in less than a week.

One more picture of the cruelty of poverty that I witnessed. I was walking through the neighborhood close to the orphanage when I came upon an accident. A young woman had been hit by a truck, and her left leg was broken, canted severely off to the left. It must have just happened, and I didn't want to stand around and gawk. I assumed the ambulance would be there soon, so I went on my way. Probably close to a year later I happened to be walking in that same neighborhood, and to my horror there I saw the same girl with the broken leg still sticking out to the left, making her a lifetime cripple for something that could have been so easily repaired.

This poverty was hopeless, ignorant and hateful, and the worst part for me, I could do nothing to change it. We came here with the notion of helping people, but early on I was seeing how huge the problems really were. If satan had his way, this is what every country in the world would be like. We thought we knew what we were doing; we came to Haiti with a plan. As often happens when my soul is crushed and broken, God puts a song in my heart to remind me that it is all about His plan, not mine. The following song was written in the winter of 1985.

THE HEART OF MAN

The problems seem so difficult, the answers hard to find.
We charge out with solutions Lord, have we left you far behind?
I can't remember asking just what you had in mind.
Oh Father, won't you forgive me one more time?
I can see the wreckage scattered all across this land,
Our good intentions fouling up your plans.
For only God can know the heart of man,
Only God can know we're in His hand,
And only God can change the heart of man.

I remember another time we were going over the mountains in the south, when I saw something that I could have changed. We came across a man with withered legs; they looked like little twisted branches that hung below his waist. He was moving up the road using two chairs. One he sat in, the other he picked up from his left side and placed it on his right side. Then he scooted onto that chair, and repeated the process over and over. He must have been heading up to a group of men conducting a chicken fight about a quarter mile up the road, I don't know. I saw this all in a matter of three or four seconds that it took to pass him by in the car. It never occurred to me until later that I should have stopped and found out his name and where he lived. A wheel chair would have changed his life. It seems that Haitians excel at enduring the most miserable hardships. What would be to us as mere pocket change could amount to days of hard labor to the average Haitian. I remember watching a man breaking round river rocks into gravel that could be used in making concrete. His wife and children carried the rocks up a steep bank from the dry riverbed in little baskets on their heads. He used part of an old engine block as an anvil, and with a short-handled mallet he would pound the rocks into crushed gravel. But the handle on the mallet was loose, and as many a time as I would see him working, he always did the same thing; he hit the rock once, twice, a third time, and then he'd have to bang the end of the handle on his anvil to retighten the head of his mallet. I can't for the life of me figure out why he never repaired the mallet. It was broken and needed to be repaired, but he just lived with it. When he had a dump truck load of crushed gravel, someone would come with the truck, and he would load the gravel onto the truck with a shovel. For all that work he received $20, while people in America whine for a $15 an hour minimum wage for flipping burgers.

Our orphanage was located just a couple blocks away from the Riviere Froide, or "Cold River." I rode over there one day on my Honda XL 600 and found a bunch of kids there with their little Suzuki 90s, some smaller, a few bigger. For the most part they don't import bikes any bigger than the Honda 125 or 250. When they saw the 600 numbers on the side of my bike, I could hear them chattering in Creole that somebody had just painted those numbers on, because they had never heard of a bike that big. But then I heard one little boy say "gade sa! Li genyon gwo machin!" "Look, it's got a big engine!" Well, when they all realized that this was really a 600, they immediately lined up in a row indicating they wanted to race so they could see what this bike would do. Well, it was one-two-three and we were off. The little two-cycle bikes jumped right out in front of everybody because they were so light. Most of the smaller bikes had gone through all five gears while I was still winding up in first gear. When I popped second gear, the front end came up and I passed the whole pack of them on the back wheel. I hung out there for a couple of hours playing with those kids, popping wheelies and giving rides. It was a fun time.

Our Five Youngest Haitian Girls

I remember another time Dave, a coworker from the orphanage, and I were out on our bikes heading for Mare Rouge, a small town in the northern peninsula. On our way he wanted to stop in a town called Gonaives to look for something, I think it was some store. We were heading down Main Street, but something didn't look right. People were just standing there watching us go by, they weren't acting normal. When we got about halfway through town, a few blocks in front of us a bunch of military men stepped out into the street, rifles at the ready, blocking our way. We didn't know what the deal was, but it seemed apparent they didn't want us going that way, so we turned around and headed back the way we had come. It seemed that every eye was upon us. Well, since I had such a great audience, I couldn't help myself. I popped a nice big wheelie, and everybody on the street just cheered and jumped and waved their arms in apparent joy. We found out later the military had been brought in to put down a rebellion over John Claude Duvalier declaring himself to be president for life. I think my little wheelie was taken as act of me flipping off the military guys.

We were coming up to Thanksgiving time, so Millie and a co-worker Sylvie rode a tap tap into town to buy a turkey along with some other supplies. They ended up with two large bags full of fruits and vegetables, and a live turkey. When they came back on the tap tap there was no place for the turkey except to stuff it under the seat. When they got out to their destination in Carrefour, it was a mile walk uphill to the orphanage. In Haiti all the women carry their burdens on their heads, so Millie and Sylvie decided they could do the same. With both bags settled nicely on top of their heads, they each grabbed a leg of the Turkey and carried it between them. Now both gals were a little on the short side, which meant they had to lift the turkey up high enough to keep it from dragging its beak in the gravel, but then their arms would get tired and pretty soon the bird would be bouncing off the ground again. About halfway up the hill the fruit in their baskets started leaking through the bag and down their faces. They finally made it up to the house and they were laughing about what they must look like to the Haitians.

They gave the Turkey to our cook, Soeur Yonik, and asked her to pluck the turkey. Millie went out after a while to see how she was doing and she saw the Turkey had been nicely plucked, except it was blinking its eyes. She hadn't killed it first! Millie was horrified and told Yonik to cut that Turkey's head off! Later, Soeur Yonik came into the kitchen and handed Millie the turkey, and it had all been cut up in little pieces. I suppose she couldn't conceive of the notion of eating the entire turkey all at one time. Just as well; it was tough as shoe leather. So much for a traditional Thanksgiving turkey.

Francois Duvalier, better known as Papa Doc, was a country doctor when he won a popular vote to the presidency in 1957. He was a tyrant who sought to keep the people poor, illiterate and superstitious. He loved voodoo and used it to help control the people after declaring himself president for life. He did not trust the military so he started his own force called the "Tonton Macoutes." The literal meaning was an "uncle with a boogie bag." It came from voodoo mythology, and it was believed he would capture children, put them in his bag and eat them later. The Macoutes were mostly a volunteer force and became the eyes and ears of the Duvaliers. They were given "privileges," and were for the most part hated by the people. By 1986 they outnumbered the Haitian army two to one. In 1961, in failing health, Papa Doc declared his only son, Jean Claude, to be president in his place. He died shortly after. Jean Claude was a worthless playboy, and at age nineteen he became the youngest president in the world.

My wife, three children and I had been in Haiti for a year and a half when Jean Claude Duvalier, aka "Baby Doc," was exiled from the country. Back in May of 1985, he had declared himself president for life, just as his father had done, and it was all downhill from there; rebellion crescendoed over the next seven months. Students in the college town of Gonaives, as an act of rebellion, walked out of classes. So, "Baby Doc" says "You don't want to go to school? Fine, I'll close the schools, all of them," which included our children's. Then he imposed a curfew on the whole city, and we had to be done with whatever we had to do and back in our house by two o'clock in the afternoon. We didn't know how bad things would get or where it would end. At first, we could hear gun shots in the night, but then all through the day as well. Finely, on February 6, 1986 he was gone. When Jean Claude Duvalier fled, the Macoutes had no standing in the new four-man military junta that took over the leadership of Haiti. For many years Haitians lived under the tyranny of the Tonton Macoutes. The retaliation against them was barbaric. Our yard boy came in one day and said he saw them using a severed head as a soccer ball. The weapon available to most was the machete, and they made horrific use of it.

Port-au-Prince erupted in revenge. Any home or business owned by friends or family of the Duvaliers was trashed and looted. K-Dis, owned by Duvalier's wife

Michele, was the only store that resembled anything like a store in the U.S, and it had been completely sacked. The floor was two feet deep in trampled merchandise that ran all the way out into the parking lot. I talked to the man who owned the only Toyota dealership in Haiti, and he told me that maybe once a month Duvalier would stop by at his dock and have a drink. "For that," he said, "it cost me my business." On that morning of Feb. 6, I watched a mob of angry men tear apart the BMW showroom that had been owned by Duvalier's father- in-law. They were stealing brand new cars and the police did nothing to stop them. Evidently, they couldn't find the keys to unlock the steering wheels and start them, so about eight or nine men would start to bounce the front end of the cars like a big basketball until the car was pointed downhill. Then someone would jump in and off he'd go with a $30,000 BMW, one happy Haitian!

Looting continued all over Port-au-Prince that day. A friend of mine bought a new $2,900 Frigidaire for $150. He said they were selling cushions separate because they had no idea what a sofa was. Revolutions are interesting. As I walked around to witness this great event, I was greeted by many smiling faces who would call out "Viva Blanc" which meant, "good for you, white guy" or something like that. We were the ones who sent the C-130 to haul Duvalier's sorry butt off the island. It was widely believed at the time that he left with up to $900,000,000 dollars. The cost of gasoline dropped a dollar per gallon, all of which had been going into Duvalier's pocket, and there was tax on the most basic commodities that served no one but him. Good riddance to yet another dictator.

In our two years spent in Haiti I would have gone nuts if it hadn't been for my banjo playing buddy, Don Barnett. He was my comic relief. He made me laugh when there was not a laugh left in the world. I got one of my best sayings from him. I don't remember what I was whining about at the time, but he came back with; "Well George, at least you know you don't hate yourself, otherwise you'd be glad you're so miserable." I have used that line more times than I can count.

Agape Flights is, the ministry that brought our mail down in a small plane to Port-au-Prince once a week. Each summer they would put on a Strawberry Festival where they would bring down 200 pounds of strawberries, (something that doesn't grow in Haiti), and have a big picnic with all the missionaries. Don and I were in charge of doing the music, so I decided to write a song. Now I must confess that at times I can have a little bit of a cynical bent, and it shows up in this song. Most missionaries working in Haiti just happened to live in Port-au-Prince, the only city with twenty-four-hour-a-day water and power. Don helped me with the words and we put them to the tune of "Okie From Muskogee." It was entitled "Delmas Missionary," Delmas being the road where we and many of the missionaries lived.

DELMAS MISSIONARY

We got electric lights and running water,
TV sets in Casablanca fans,
We got lots of grocery stores to spend our money,
And we ride around in air-conditioned vans.

I've got a big old house with lots of indoor plumbing,
Servants there to clean and wash my duds,
I got a brand-new Rocky sitting in the driveway,
In case I run across the little mud.

Once I took a trip to Mole St. Nichols
To bless them folks with a song or two.
But they didn't seem to appreciate my singing,
Like the people back in good old Delmas do.

Chorus
Well, I'm proud to be a Delmas missionary
Where you can have your cake and eat it too.
Its awful tough being in foreign missions
But if you keep praying brother, I'll make it through

The biggest smiles came from those who were working out in the villages. They were the ones driving the old beat up two-wheel drive pickups.

Don and I had the opportunity to go out with the "Jesus Film" to a remote part of the island. They had all the equipment, a generator, PA set, and a portable stage with intensely bright halogen lights. Between reels, I think there were four, Don and I would play guitar and banjo and lead them in singing. Well first of all it's hot, performing on stage makes it hotter, but those halogen lights were over the top hot. But the worst part was the lights drew these little black beetles out of the jungle by the thousands. They would OD on the lights, and then come raining down on Don and I. Here we were, sweating profusely with these beetles crawling down our neck and up our backs under our shirts. When the beetles got to where the guitar and banjo straps went across our backs, they couldn't get through, so they started digging. It was awful! With sweat pouring down my face and about to panic I looked over at Don. He just gave me a big smile and said "Well George, I think this is what they call suffering for Jesus!"

Don was in Haiti to teach and train the indigenous pastors, a most valuable Christian ministry. Haiti has been crawling with missionaries for the last hundred years. It's a cheap and easy country to get into, and we come thinking we know what they need. We show up with rice and beans, clothes and money, all kinds of things, feeling really good about ourselves, and we have no idea what harm we've done. The gospel of Christ has been polluted. To the average Haitian it means salvation in Jesus and some good thing at the hand of the missionary. Another friend of mine explained it this way; Haiti is like a pit of suffering, and people with the best of intentions have thrown in ropes of medical aid, others ropes of education and ropes of food, money, and yes ropes of orphanages. But Jesus is the only rope that can pull Haiti out of the pit it has been in for so long. Do you remember the story of the siege of Samaria found in 2Kings 6:24-29? The famine was so bad that two women were eating their own babies, and then in the next chapter there were four lepers who were starving to death. Now what if we did have a time machine? We would go back with food and doctors, right? But it was their depraved condition that drove them out of the city and into God's salvation.

As a Christian, our focus is first on the spiritual poverty, then the physical poverty. Jesus never went out to give food to the poor. He came to seek and to save the lost, and to spread the good news of the gospel. A few times he fed the multitudes, but it was secondary to his teaching. There are many needful humanitarian works in the country, and if you want to go feed hungry people you will never run out of them, ever. But Jesus said "The poor shall always be with you," because this poverty is the evidence of a spiritually bankrupt condition. When we were in Haiti there were about six million people there. Now there are over ten million. Are they in any way better off? Mercy and wisdom seem to be at odds here. We had no idea what we were getting into or what to do once we got there. *"We charge out with solutions Lord, have we left you far behind?"*

About a month after Duvalier was exiled, we got a call from an old woman in the states asking if it was safe to return to Haiti. We told her things were just fine. So, she asked if we could pick her up at the airport. We got her flight number and time of arrival. A missionary friend had left a luxury car with us for safe keeping when he fled the country. He said to go ahead and drive it once in a while. Since we hadn't used it at all, I told Millie we should drive it to the airport. The day came and we headed off. On the way we noticed something was different. People were not moving about in the normal way. They were milling around and hanging in groups of four or five, many holding the old Haiti flag of red and blue. Papa Doc had loved voodoo so much he had changed the flags color to black and red, as black was the color for voodoo. The crowds got bigger the closer we came to the airport. We asked some people we passed what was going on. They told us that some high-ranking Tonton Macoutes had dressed up like nuns and tried to board an Air France flight. Only problem, someone found out and reported it to Radio Soleil, and a great mob descended on the Port-au-Prince airport. With rocks, clubs, and machetes they pulled up the chain link fence and headed out for that multi-million-dollar Air France jet. The military used tear gas and water cannon to push the mob back off the tarmac. We arrived shortly after.

As we approached the terminal we could see hundreds of people on the roof, on stairs and hanging from windows. The crowd parted and allowed our car to move the last 200 yards to the main entrance. We had no fear because we were white, but the stupid luxury car was another matter.

We rolled down the windows and turned off the air conditioning so we were sweating right along with the rest of them. I knew Millie would be safer outside, so I told her to go see if the old woman was ready to go. I watched as she squeezed herself into the crowd. Just then a clearing opened up right in front of me, and thirty or forty men were standing a car up onto its front bumper, it tottered there for a moment, and then came smashing down on its top. I found out later it was the car that brought the Tonton Macoutes to the airport. It was a fancy car just like the one I was in and I didn't want to be next, so if it was possible to tip toe in a car, I did it. I got out as fast as the crowd would let me move and parked 300 yards away. I was the only white guy there and must have looked like a kernel of popcorn in that sea of angry black faces. That I was looking for someone must have been obvious, because three or four arms shot up at once with fingers pointing out Millie's location. Sometimes you just have to love those Haitians. Here they were hot, angry, all tear gassed up and ready to kill, and yet they were willing to help me find my little five-foot-two white woman. Amazing! The walkway leading to the exit doors was covered with glass from all the broken windows. Millie pointed out our passenger looking terrified, standing at the end of a customs table. She came over to us with a small suitcase and handed it out through a hole in the glass door. Just then all hell broke loose!

Four or five semiautomatic rifles opened up no more than thirty feet away. The sound was deafening, reverberating within the concrete alcove. We could feel the concussion from the muzzle blast hit our chest, and people were falling down everywhere. We thought we were dead or soon would be. Then I noticed a group of frightened young men on their feet and looking for someplace to escape from the gun fire. Millie was on the sidewalk in front of the doors. A Haitian had fallen across her back, and she was trying to hold a woman's face up out of the broken glass. I thought if the young men tried to escape into the terminal, Millie could be trampled to death, so I reached over and grabbed her shirt by the collar and dragged her through the glass over next to the wall. Then the most amazing thing happened; I felt like I was being immersed in peace from my head all the way down to my feet. My fear was completely gone. I turned to Millie and said; "A thousand may fall at your side, and ten thousand at your right hand; but it shall not come near you." (Ps. 91:7). I had never memorized that verse. I stood up and saw an army six by six pulling away from the building; they must have extracted the Tonton Macoutes from inside the airport and were trying to get away. Rocks, sticks, shoes, and whatever they had to throw was raining down on them from the roof of the airport, and the military was shooting over their heads trying to make them stop. I looked to my right and there stood a man I hadn't noticed before. He was frozen in place and looked like a white man. I asked him in creole "Eske ou renmen jezi?" Do you love Jesus? He said "Oui, Oui," as he vigorously shook both my hands. Then right in front of my eyes his color changed, and he turn back into a black man. What a crazy day that was!

One day my six- year- old son, Daniel, and I were heading back to the orphanage on my motorcycle, a 600 Honda XL. We didn't have helmets. The road going out to Carrefour was a two lane which didn't mean a lot; we have seen four lines of traffic going in one direction on that narrow road. There were a few personal vehicles, but for the most part the "tap tap" was the only public means of transportation. There were hundreds of them. There were no central points to pick up or drop off the people like our bus routes have, which means they could be expected to pull over anywhere, at any moment, without notice. Then in the same manner they would pull right out in front of you; that's why in Haiti you cannot drive a car without a horn, preferably a really loud one. Sharing the road with all this are burros laden with produce and charcoal, and these big two-wheeled carts pulled by one or more men. I once saw two men pulling a cart with twenty-seven bags of Portland cement on it; that's 2,538 pounds!

At any rate, Dan and I were on our way home when a tap tap pulled right out in front of us. Since there was no oncoming traffic I started to pass, but then the diver of the tap tap pulled out to the left to go around a cart. Well now I can't see what's coming, so I snapped the throttle open and shot past the tap tap. My speed had jumped to fifty miles per hour as I cleared the tap tap, when I saw it, a death trap. There was a passenger car stopped on the far end of a narrow bridge waiting to make a left turn. It was canted a little to the left in preparation for the turn. A five-ton truck was approaching in the oncoming lane. Here is where a picture is worth a thousand words, but I'll do my best to describe it. I was coming into this mess at the worst possible time. I could see I would get to the car at the same time as the truck. I had hit the brakes and the back tire was already locked up; I couldn't stop in time. There was not enough room between the car and the bridge to go to the right, and if I tried to go left, I would run head on into the truck. I was going to hit the car at a very sharp angle, which would slide us right out in front of the truck. This was a no-win situation and I was out of time. I was going to hit just back of the driver's door. Your body's fight/flight response to panic is to dump a ton of adrenalin into your blood stream; this causes your brain to go into warp drive. So, I had all the time in the world to consider the outcome of this collision. Somehow, I knew for a certainty two things; one, that I was going to live, and two, I was going to lose my only son. This took all of three or four seconds, but it seemed like I had hours to grieve over what was about to happen. I can still recall the profound sadness I had time to feel. I closed my eyes and gritted my teeth just as we hit the car then; NOTHING HAPPENED! I opened my eyes in shock, and found us going down the road on the other side of the car just as normal as you please. I looked back and saw the car still waiting to make its turn. No way in the world could I have made it through that, this was a FULL-BLOWN MIRACLE. Someday I hope I'll get to see the rerun on that one. Thank you, thank you, thank you Jesus…

We came to Haiti to manage an orphanage, but out of forty children only two were orphans, the rest had parents and siblings in the neighborhood. The kids were in our house because of poverty, their parents couldn't feed them. We raised them like little Americans with running water, servants to cook and clean, refrigeration, electric lights, and three meals a day. Something unattainable for over seventy percent of the population. Was it fair to introduce them to a life style they might never live to afford? But a Christian school with a feeding program could have accomplished the same thing for less money and kept the kids in their own culture.

We had found an outreach called Christianville which had been in country six years longer than we had. They started in 1978 with an orphanage similar to ours, but then they grew into what it is today a school with a feeding program and many other programs. They are a great ministry in Haiti. If you're looking for something worth supporting, I would highly recommend Christianville.

I don't mean to say that all orphanages are a bad idea. In some parts of the world because of certain conditions it is the only solution. There was an attempt to change gears and start a mission in the northern part of Haiti, but I could not see myself as a needed player in what was coming. We returned to Washington State carrying the load of this failed endeavor. We had no job waiting, a house or even a car. All I had was a vision I received at our house in Port au Prince. I was having one of those heart wrenching "what do I do now" talks with God, when he brought to mind a picture of the western half of the U.S. There was a red light in the middle of the Bitterroot Valley of Western Montana. That was all I had to go on, and within two weeks we were on our way to Montana, "going home to a place we'd never been before."

If we could use a time machine to go back two hundred years in the United States, we would find most Americans had large families, living in small houses with no electricity, no running water, and no refrigeration. And like todays Haitians; many could not read or write. So why are the Haitians stuck in the past? It's the poorest nation in the western hemisphere. What is responsible for this heritage of poverty they keep passing down to the next generations? It's a complicated question. They started out as slaves. In 1804 they ran their French captors off the island, winning their independence. It was the only successful slave revolution in the western world. But what became the ruling class were the fair skinned offspring of the French Africans. The mulattos were the only ones with any education or training. And they were as self-serving as their French captors had been. America was still a slave state in 1804, and there was no way we would help with this new nation. We didn't recognize Haiti until the start of the civil war in 1862.

But we had something 200 years ago that the people of Haiti did not have; Christianity. J.J. Dessalines, one of four generals involved in the early defense of Haiti, reasoned with his contemporaries that they could not call upon the God of Napoleon to come to their aid. So instead, they turned to their gods of Africa. In a solemn ceremony they sacrificed a pig to the animistic embrace of Voodoo as their national religion. There was a bronze statue of a pig in front of the national post office to commemorate this event. The underlying tenet of Christianity is; "Do unto others as you would have them do unto you," the teaching of the Good Samaritan. "Look not unto your own needs, but look to the needs of others." (Phil. 2:4). If you wish to be a leader, become a servant. The Bible goes on and on in this theme, and it has shaped our nation in a very positive way.

Voodoo on the other hand is wholly devoid of any such notions. On one end it's a very long list of benign charms, like our lucky rabbit's foot, four leaf clover, or walking under a ladder. But there is a darker side of houngan priests preforming ritual sacrifices, calling on a multitude of spirits to possess or mount them. There is much more that could be said about voodoo, but my point is this; Voodoo does nothing to create good citizens. There are no good Samaritans woven into the fabric of Haitian society. They have no revered national heroes who sacrificed themselves for the good of their countrymen. Elected officials once in power have nine times out of ten used it to enrich themselves. The poor of Haiti have never had their day in the sun.

What is the solution for Haiti, since we seem to be fresh out of time machines? I can't get my head around it, "the problems seem so difficult, the answers hard to find." It would be wonderful if they could find a truly great Christian leader. They've never had one you know, someone like Hezekiah who pulled down the high places and destroyed the evil priests.

One of my favorite song writers, Ken Medema, wrote the following; *"Is there a place for dreaming in the corners of your mind, in a world where dreams are broken and dreamers hard to find. Do you dream and weep sometimes about the way that things should be? Come dreaming with me, dreaming with me, admission is free."*

Please pray for Haiti, pray for a dream of righteousness to grow in the hearts of Christian men and women in Haiti.

CHAPTER 16
FINDING HOME

On the long flight back from Port-au-Prince, Haiti, to Washington state, I had plenty of time to reflect on the last two years. This was a poorly-conceived missionary project and, in the end, it affected a number of people in a negative way. When I was first approached with the notion of the orphanage, I was halfway through a course at A T&T Technical Institute. It was all paid for. However, the need was imminent and I was encouraged to "pray about going to Haiti." For a long time, it had been my earnest desire to serve the Lord in any way I could. I said "Okay." Looking out the window at the clouds below, I considered the notion of asking the church to return me to my original condition. *"Well,"* I thought, *"That's not very realistic, and besides there is an old axiom of the law that states 'He who consents to an act is not wronged by it.'"* (The Volenti Maxim.)

I think we had to change planes in Denver, and then continued on to PDX in Portland. I was taking inventory on what we needed to do. First off, what we didn't have was a house, a job, a car, or money, but what we did have was our destination; the little red light in the middle of the Bitterroot Valley of Western Montana. That's all we had to go on. It took two weeks to finalize our affairs in Vancouver. Some very good friends saw our plight and bought a used station wagon for us, and the church gave us $1000. We said goodbye to friends and family, and headed up the Columbia River gorge east toward Montana.

Stevensville was about dead center of the Bitterroot Valley, and when we pulled into town there was not a car on the road, just two horses tied up to a fire hydrant in front of the Lonesome Dove Saloon. Well, I thought this looked perfect. We stopped at a real estate office and ended up buying the first piece of property we were shown, a twenty-acre irrigated parcel on the east side of the valley. Economically speaking, things were very poor in the Bitterroot Valley. But I had a job offer as a supervisor at the Stapleton Airport in Denver, CO. My brother lived just east of Denver. I don't remember for sure now, but I think he was the one who put my name in the hat for that job.

We rented a small house in the town of Bennett, east of Denver. I took the job at the airport, Millie found a job in home health care, and our three kids got enrolled at the local school, which was about to start. The job at the airport wasn't hard. We oversaw about seventy drivers who drove the shuttles to and from the airport and the airport-owned parking lots. Drugs and alcohol use among our drivers was one of our biggest problems. There were also some occasional fender benders, no big deal.

However, my work schedule was a problem. In every single week I worked two day shifts, two swing shifts, and one graveyard shift, all in the same week. What kind of sadist thought that schedule up I'll never know! But I could not sleep, and I tried everything I could think of. I taped aluminum foil up to the windows to try to shut out the light, and left the air conditioner running just to make background noise, but nothing helped. I just couldn't sleep. I fought this for three whole months before I just got to the point where I couldn't put up with it anymore, and I quit. Then I spent the next three months looking for a job. There were lots of jobs to be had, but they were all $5-an hour jobs, and we couldn't make it on that. Finally, I told Millie we couldn't keep paying rent here and making land payments in Montana. I said we either need to let the land go, or I need to go up there and get some kind of a house up for us, to move into when school was out in the spring. Millie said *"GO! I would rather starve to death on my own property."*

I arrived in Montana on March 11, 1987. It was cold! There was a water well close to the road, which meant I had electricity, and that was good. Also, there was a septic system on the property. I had $650 from our tax return to build the house with. So, I started looking for cheap lumber. A man named Phil Johnson had a lumber yard in Missoula that sold economy two-by-fours for fifty cents apiece, and half-inch plywood blows - that's plywood with places that didn't get glued. I can't remember what I paid for them, not much. I started with the idea of building something small that we could later on use as a storage shed. I settled on a twelve-by-twenty-foot structure that we could sort of camp in, and if necessary, store our stuff in while we went looking for work somewhere else. I started building it up next to the pumphouse because I had power there. Also, I put it on skids so I could move it wherever I wanted. A friend stopped by and told me I should make the roof a 12/12 pitch, and that would give enough head room for a small loft, a good idea because tiny as it was, it became a bedroom for our two daughters.

I started out just sleeping in the car, but it was really getting cold, so somebody gave me a portable oil heater to use. That worked okay, but I had to leave the windows rolled down to keep from getting asphyxiated. This put me close to a zero net gain on heating things up. I had started going to a little church called Light of The Valley, down in Stevensville. When they heard of my plight, they offered me a couch in a heated room that was only used on Sundays for a classroom; that was a big improvement. It didn't end there. When the ladies of the church realized they had a young man who was nearly starved to death, they started feeding me like there was no tomorrow. So, I had a warm place to stay, lots food to eat, and cheap lumber to build with. What more did I need?

Finding Home

I had decided to hitchhike the 650 miles back to Vancouver, WA, to get an old Ford pickup and a small tractor we still had there. When the pastor of the church heard what I was about to do, he talked the church into paying for a railroad ticket for me. Thank you, good people! The passenger railroad station was up in Whitefish, and the train left in the middle of the night, which gave that pastor a five-hour round-trip drive to get me up there. I don't find anything in the vault concerning that trip, so I must have slept most of the way. I do remember on the way back to Montana I had stopped at a gas station, and I noticed a guy examining the old cub tractor I had in the back of the truck. He seemed quite interested, and at last he asked if I was taking the tractor to a museum. Well, I thought that was funny, and I told him the tractor wasn't going into retirement, it was going to work in Montana. We stood there talking for a good ten minutes, and I pointed out how the seat, steering wheel and cultivators were all off center on the right side of the tractor. This tractor was designed and built for row crop farming. When you were seated with the cultivators down in position, the row you were cultivating ran right between your feet, so it was very easy to see what you were doing. I don't think a half a dozen rototillers could keep up with what this little twelve-horsepower tractor could do. There's just nothing out there like this old International Cub.

The Vault

George and Teddy on the International Cub Tractor

The man we had purchased the twenty acres from was named Stan Hendrickson. He was a very likable, easygoing fellow, and sported a smile for almost every occasion. Stan bought and sold just about everything under the sun. I remember him telling me about four boxes of nails he had just bought at auction for little or nothing. They were an odd size nail, somewhere in the neighborhood of a five-penny nail. He fished one out of a box and went to the local hardware store. When He found the owner, a man he knew, he asked him if he had any nails like this, handing him the nail. He looked at it, rolled it between his thumb and forefinger, and he said *"Sorry, I don't have anything this size."* Stan said, *"Well, how would you like to buy some? I have four cases you can have for a hundred dollars."* Now that was a good price! Stan was obviously happy with himself over this deal, because he didn't have to do so much as lift the box. He told the store owner they were down at the auction house, and he walked away with a $100 bill. Stan was one of those guys who made more money by accident than I ever made on purpose.

I was progressing on with what we all came to call the birdhouse. Because of the dimensions, it looked just like a birdhouse, only bigger. I was telling a friend that I should nail the lid of a fifty-five-gallon drum up on the end of the house to look like the hole the bird came in and out of, then put up a fence post for the perch. I had all the plywood nailed up, plus a reclaimed door and window, so it was time to move the house about 200 feet to the west, so we would be away from the dust from the gravel road. It was around this time that a neighbor named Linda stopped by to welcome me to the neighborhood and to say hello. She and her husband, Barry, lived about a half-mile away, and became very good friends for many years. When it came time to move the house, I used round wooden fence posts as rollers, and I laid pieces of scrap wood on the ground for the posts to roll on. With the pickup hooked up to the front of the house, I started pulling. As fence posts would roll out from the back end of the house, people helping me would run around to reset the posts at the front end of the skids. It worked great. In no time at all, I had the bird house moved to its permanent location. I leveled the house up on cinder blocks placed about five feet apart on the two rails. Thirty-five years later, that house is still sitting on those cinder blocks. A few days later, Linda stopped by to see how I was doing, but she was a little puzzled about the house's new location. She said *"Didn't that house used to be up there?"* (Pointing back to the pump house). Without missing a beat, I said *"Oh yes, but I wanted to move it closer to the mountains so I could see them better."* She said with a puzzled look on her face *"Oh, I see."*

The twenty-acre parcel was sold with a well and a septic system. It turned out that the septic system had to be replaced, so Stan showed up with his backhoe to put in a brand-new system. While he was there, I had him dig in the water line from the well to the birdhouse. The inside of the house was still just bare studs, but I had a Coleman stove and lantern, and a few lawn chairs. It was quite homey. Stan and I were sitting in the house, and as we were talking, he told me he would trade everything he had to change places with me, just starting out like I was. That was a big encouragement to me, the first sign that I was getting somewhere on this new Montana project.

The $650 that I brought with me to Montana was long gone. I would have to stop construction on the house and go work somewhere for five bucks an hour. I remember telling Millie back in Denver that we couldn't live on five bucks an hour. Now I'm trying to build a house and live on five bucks an hour. But as Millie said, at least we're starving to death on our own property. When I got some cash in my pocket, I would go buy some insulation, sheet rock or wiring to put in the house. I remember doing a lot of work for a guy named Louis. He lived about three miles from the house. I built fencing, did some painting, built a stone platform under his wood stove, all for five bucks an hour. But he and his wife, Rose, cooked the best lunches in the world! They would chatter on like Chip n' Dale as they worked in the kitchen. I didn't want to waste the gas to drive over there, so I would walk the three miles to save a little money. Louis made a big fuss over me having to walk all that way. It troubled him some, but not enough to budge him up on what he was paying me.

It was warming up a little, so I had moved into the birdhouse full time. By the end of May I had all the wiring, insulation, and sheet rocking done. I did some work for Stan where I learned how to do taping and mudding, so I was able to do that as well. The walls were all painted, and I covered the two-by-four rafters with one-and-a-half-inch Styrofoam panels, so it was looking pretty good. But who was I fooling? It was only a twelve-by-twenty-foot room, so I started the first of four lean-tos. By the time I went to get Millie and the kids down in Colorado, I had an eight-by-twelve floor with two walls standing, including a toilet. You had to stand a sheet of plywood up for privacy.

Here again, Stan came to the rescue with the offer of himself, his truck, and a twenty-six-foot gooseneck trailer. He and I went to pick up Millie, the kids, and all of our stuff, plus four goats and two cats, down in Bennett, Colorado. We put my car up on the trailer going down, and Stan and I jabbered all the way to Colorado; he was good company. I remember he wanted $400 to cover the cost of the fuel, which was a pretty cheap way to move up to Montana. I think he was so used to people not paying up on what they owed him, because when I was finally able to get the money to him, he almost looked like he was going to cry.

I watched Stan back the trailer up to the front door of the birdhouse. Even with the first lean-to started, the trailer was almost the exact same size as the house. I thought, *"I guess we're going to need more lean-tos."* Millie needed a kitchen, and since 12x20 seemed to work so well the first time, I thought we would make this lean-to the same size as the house. Here again, money was in short supply, but we had lots of rocks laying around, big piles of them. I thought, *"Why not use rocks for the floor and the footings?"* I found out about a neighbor who had sand that was clean enough to be used in mortar mix. I had to shovel it into the truck by hand, but I got it for free. We all worked for a month and a half building that stone floor and stem wall. Daniel shoveled sand. Gale and Jennifer sieved the sand and made mortar. Millie was finding the right sized rocks, and I was the self-taught mason, laying rocks flat side up. The biggest area we completed in one day was approximately 4x6 feet. It took forever to build that rock floor, but in the end, what started as an act of desperation ended up being one of the most attractive features of that little house.

That first Christmas, we went up into the mountains and found a beautiful tree that we brought home and put up in our little house. We didn't have any ornaments to put on the tree, so Millie crocheted a bunch of white snowflakes, and an angel for the top of the tree. The kids made a bunch of little characters out of cotton balls and stuff they got from school. The stars and all the things the kids made are still the first ornaments to go on the tree, even today after all these years.

By the end of the second year Millie had a wood cookstove, and we heated with wood. The house was warm and comfy, and everybody had a place to sleep, just barely. We had a cow named Moo, who came with a mortgage. Millie made cheese and butter, and we had all the milk we could drink. We had a horse, a dog, two cats, chickens, and a very large garden. For the second time in our married lives, everything on our plates was what we grew or raised. It was a good feeling. In the garden we were strictly organic, and that can make things harder. For example, our potatoes had a bad infestation of Colorado potato beetle, and there was no organic spray for them. So, the five of us spread out in the potato patch with an empty can, and we just picked the bugs off the plants and put them in the can. When the can was full, you just dumped them into a five-gallon bucket half full of water and drowned the little rascals. Actually, I didn't mind just squishing them between my thumb and forefinger. I could use both hands and do it a lot faster. Another problem we had in the garden was quack grass, and unless you used Roundup, there was no easy way to get rid of it. If you wanted to be organic, you had three options. Number one, cover the ground with some sort of plastic sheeting, leave it on there for a whole year, and that will kill it. Or you could just keep the ground tilled up for a whole year, and that would kill it also. But these two options took a long time, and we didn't have a long time; we needed to grow food now. So, we did it the hard way. I would plow one furrow full length of the garden and turn the tractor off. Then the five of us would spread out along the furrow, and using our hands, we would pick the quack grass rhizomes out of the soil. It took a long time, but it did the trick.

I had the soil tested, and found out that the pH was very high, I think around eight, so it had to come down. We found some natural sulfur soil that did the trick, and we had the best potatoes we have ever grown using that sulfur soil (no scabs). I needed one more thing, and I knew where to get it. The how to get it was something I had to give some thought to, because you can only expect so much from your kids.

About midweek after school, I started telling the kids that we were going to do an activity we had never done before, and it was going to have something to do with food. Each day I would add a little more intrigue, so by the time we got to Saturday morning they were actually excited about whatever it was we were going to do. They followed me as I drove our pickup through the gate, out into the pasture. Millie was listening to the girls chatter about what it might be. Then she heard our youngest daughter Jennifer say, *"Oh no! I know what it's going to be. He's going to make us pick up cowpies."* Our oldest daughter Gale said *"No, he wouldn't do that."* But Jennifer was right. Last summer I had leased the twenty acres out to eighteen cow/calf pairs, which meant there were a lot of dried cow pies, easy to pick up. Think of them as organic frisbees. Well, what followed was a half day of absolute hilarity. They started out a bit sullen as you would expect, but as the day progressed, the kids started doing what kids do, making fun out of it. There were several "chip wars," and who could throw the chip the farthest and still hit the pickup. Then they would come back to the pickup with armloads of cowpies. We were all laughing the whole day, but the best part was this song the kids made up; *"Picking up cowpies, thro'em in the pickup, picking up cowpies, thro'em in the pickup."* I wish I had a picture of us coming back with our last load, the kids, all three of them, sitting on top of the cow poo pile singing that song.

I finally got hired on at a welding shop in the town of Stevensville. I had tried a number of times to get hired on, but because I had never run dual shield, (that was a type of wire used in welding), the supervisor would not hire me. So, one day I showed up with my tool bag and leathers, and told the gal at the front desk *"I am here to take the test."* Well, she didn't know anything about it, so she called the foreman off the floor, and he must have assumed I had been called in for a test. So, he set me up at a machine to run my test plates. I welded the plates, they put them through a bender to test my weld, and it passed. So, I went upstairs to the supervisor with my test plates, set them on his desk, and told him I wanted the job now. What could he do? He gave me the job. My last welding job in Vancouver paid over $15 an hour, and that was good money at the time. Five years later they offered me $7.50 an hour here in the Bitterroot. It was $2.50 more than

I made working for "Screwy Louie." I only stayed with the welding shop for thirteen months.

Have you ever seen a bunch of cows go down to drink water out of a pond? They don't just stop at the water's edge and drink; no sir, they'll go stomping all over the pond, stirring up mud with each step, and then when they've made a complete mess, they drink the muddy water. That's kind of the way it was down at the welding shop. I mean it was bad enough getting up at 4:30 in the morning, making a lunch and eating breakfast, to be anywhere by 6 o'clock. But welding shops stink by nature, the welding fumes, the grinding, the cutting and the banging on steel. It was bad enough all by itself. But there were some guys who, like the cows, found ways to make it worse, a back biting, foul mouthed bunch of ingrates.

I have to say, the first two years was an act of desperation. But that all changed one day as if by magic. A man a little younger than I stopped by for a visit. He was a fellow worker at the welding shop. He lived in a rented mobile home about ten miles south of me. I wish I could remember his name, for he changed my entire perspective in almost a supernatural way. I showed him around our farm that we had created. When he saw all the animals, the garden, the house, and the barn, with pure undeniable honesty he exclaimed *"You have got it made!"* He was so sincere about my status in life, and it changed everything. From that day on I realized I had won the fight. It was revolutionary. It's not that I had lost hope, but I had forgotten about hope, and thankfulness.

Finding Home

I had pulled so hard and so long in the harness, I forgot to stop and look back to see what I had plowed. So, I took a job driving a propane truck for the next four years. Just me and the truck, we got along fine, and it paid better.

We made what was at that time a large purchase. We bought a good quality trampoline, and it was the best investment we ever made. Everybody played on that for hours, it was good exercise, and nobody was ever seriously injured. The kids played on that for years and years, and when they were all moved out of the house, it went first to one kid's house and then to another.

Daniel, Gale and Jennifer on Trampoline

CHAPTER 17
"WE ALL GOT A ROW TO HOE"

When we first started to look into the vault "safely hidden in a labyrinth of neurons," it was never my intention to write about my kids, but rather to them. I would have loved to know more about my father, but as I have already stated, I hardly knew him. So, I wanted to tell my kids how I came to be. Now that this is becoming a book, I need to back up a little and write about the kids, starting with our girls. There will be more about our son a little further on. Among the contents of the vault, I had used words like "funny, happy, and hilarious." Kids can generate boxes full of that kind of material in a single day.

The first thing I need to say is how different our daughters Gale and Jennifer were one from the other. The girls were born only fourteen months apart, but they could not have been more different. I would be tempted to say different as dogs and cats, but I don't like cats, so I can't use that one. They were more like a general practitioner and a specialist. A general practitioner can stitch up your knee when it gets kissed by a chainsaw, diagnose and treat a bladder infection, or write you a prescription for antibiotics. They are very useful for a lot of things. A specialist, however, is just what its name implies, special. They pick what they want to do in life, and that's what they do. The difference between the two could be clearly seen when out in the garden. They both had a row to hoe, only one per day. Gale, our general practitioner, would go like a house afire down her row and get it all weeded in about twenty minutes. She would miss a few, but not bad for a GP.

Our little specialist, Jennifer, on the other hand always zeroed in on the tiny. With her little nose only inches from the ground, she would find the tiniest, almost microscopic little weeds growing among the plants. She didn't seem to mind that it took her two or three times as long to do her row, she was just happy being herself. We would often find her all doubled over looking at the tiniest little flower and exclaiming how cute it was. *"Look! It has five little stems in the middle of the flower."* Well, standing there looking down I could barely see the flower, let alone the stamen inside the flower. Another story I like to tell is about the rabbit beans. She doesn't like this story because I've told it so many times. I had to get her permission to use it. It all started on a day when I was very busy, and passing by Jennifer out in the backyard, I asked her to clean up under the rabbit hutch and put the manure out in the garden. Well, she presented herself to me about three hours later to say that she had finished. This really piqued my interest, because the whole job could not have taken more than twenty minutes, so I had to investigate. First, I went and looked under the rabbit hutch, and I noted that the corrugated metal I had underneath to catch the droppings was almost spotless. That would have taken some time, but not three hours. I went out to the garden to see where she dumped it, and I found to my surprise and amazement that she had placed exactly four beans around each and every plant in the whole garden. I mean, that there is a specialist!

Another day I was putting a roof on a shed that was right next to the garden, and the girls were out hoeing their rows. But this day they were bickering with each other. It got so bad I finally told them to knock it off. They stopped for a bit, but then were back at it again. Finally, I told them they were going to get a spanking. I was too busy to come down off the roof, so I told them they would have to give it to themselves. Here's where funny and hilarious come in. At first, the oldest one thought that was kind of funny, but as they were spanking their own behinds, I told them to do it harder, HARDER. Well, pretty soon they were crying their eyes out like they were getting the beating of their life. We all knew they were putting on a show.

Raising good kids is not that difficult, all you need is consistency and common sense. Start them out young and give them their own "row to hoe," whatever that might be. "Train up a child in the way he should go and when he is old, he will not depart from it." Proverbs 22:6. I'm very proud of my three children. They are all straight arrows, and are doing a better job of raising their children than

I did with them. They're the kind of people other people want for friends.

We processed all of our own meat, whether it be chickens, goats, beef, venison or sheep. It wasn't anybody's favorite job; it was just something that had to be done. I remember one day when I was processing two sheep. The first one was tame, and I could walk right up to it. I popped it in the back of the head with my 380 semi-automatic pistol, and down it went. After I'd finished with the first one, I went to do the second one. But it had seen what happened to the first one, and wasn't going without a fight. It was running round and round inside the corral trying to stay away from me. I went for a headshot as it was running by, and I saw the bullet ricochet off its head, going straight up in the air. I saw that the slide on my pistol was locked back, which meant I was out of ammo. So now I would have to go back to the house and get more ammo for the gun, then come back and finish the job. But I looked at the sheep, and it was just standing there. I walked over to look at it and there was no mark on his head where the bullet had hit, but it was knocked out cold standing on its feet. I waved my hand in front of its face and gave it a little nudge. Nothing! I thought, *"That's good enough for me."* I pulled out my knife and cut its throat. As luck would have it, at that very moment Millie walked out to the corral to see how I was doing; she didn't know the sheep was unconscious. *"What are you doing!"* she cried out.

Oh boy! Now I know I have been very tough on some of you vegetarians that might be reading this, or those who think their lamb chops come from the cooler at the Safeway store, but this is how it's done. I'm sorry.

Back in Haiti when I was having that heart-to-heart talk with God, and He showed me the little red light in the middle of the Bitterroot Valley, I thought He was sending me here to do some great missionary work. But no, God sent me here to raise our children, now to the third generation. We came here with nothing, now we have everything. Here is a song we have been singing together all of our lives, because it fits us to a "T." I wish I had written it; it is called

HUMPBACK MULE

Thank you, thank you, thank you, Lord, for all you've done for me.
I'm richer now than any man has any right to be
Health and love and happiness have been my cup of tea
The richest man in all creation surely envies me.

Chorus: I've got a humpback mule, plough, and a tater patch
Eggs that are gonna hatch some day
Got the Lord above and a good girl to love me
I'm the richest man in the world.

I don't have much bank account, my cash on hand is small
But tell me what are riches but contentment, after all

The Vault

**Other folks may think I'm poor, but I know that's not so
For when I count my blessings, I'm the richest
man I know.
Chorus:**

I do consider myself one of the richest men I know.

I'm spending a lot of time in the vault trying to sort out all the different colors, different feelings, the failures, the successes. The first two or three years in Montana were difficult. I haven't looked into this part of the vault for some years. We tend to spend more time looking at the "happy days." In this period of time, I find little bits and pieces, really a record of efforts that I made trying to make some money. I was desperate. We tried a small commercial greenhouse, raising garlic to sell, and I even tried making soap. Nothing was working. I even sent away for a home study course in business. The only one who made money on that deal was the guy that sold it to me. We got involved in a new real estate dealership called "By Owner." It was a new concept where people paid for an advertising package up front instead of paying a much bigger percentage at the time of sale. The concept did not go over too well, because at that time land had just not been selling, and people didn't want to put money up front for a sale that may not happen. We also ran a take-and-bake pizza parlor, and a video rental next door to the real estate office. But it was like we were invisible, because nobody stopped by. Even with weekly radio and newspaper ads, people just seemed to ignore us.

It might have been because the buildings that we rented had not been used in years, and people just sort of drove by and didn't even notice that something else was going on in there. We ate a lot of pizza.

The farm was doing great, but we had done that sort of thing before, and we knew what we were doing. One thing that we really needed though was a good root cellar, something to protect the produce of our garden from freezing. Our land had flood irrigation, so you couldn't just dig a hole in the ground and frame it in because it would fill up with water. We tried using our pumphouse, which was insulated and had a heat lamp, to keep things from freezing up. The only trouble with that is, when the electricity went out, we lost everything that was in the pumphouse, including the pump. We needed something we could put in the ground that would be water tight.

I came up with a perfect solution. I found a discarded fuel tank, the kind used at filling stations. Most of the tanks were 30,000 gallons in size, which were eight feet high and almost thirty feet long. It was a lot of work. First, they had to be cut open using an Acetylene torch. DO NOT TRY THIS YOURSELF!!! If you don't do a proper job of venting the tank, you will blow yourself into the next century. Then I would use a power washer to clean the inside of the tank. With two-by-two angle iron and plywood, I made the floor and the shelves. In my tank, I also made a cot that came in handy on hot summer days for a cool nap. If you can get the top of your tank five feet underground, the temperature in the tank will stay pretty consistent year around, cool in the summer and warm in the winter.

A good friend and neighbor, Donnie, had helped me build my tank. When he saw how well it worked, he decided to build one for himself. Then other people started seeing our root cellars, and they wanted them too. So, for about ten or fifteen years, Donnie and I built root cellars for people all over the valley. We got all the tanks we needed for free, because there was a federal mandate that stated all single-walled fuel tanks had to be out of the ground by, I think it was 1998. A lot of the older tanks had rusted through in places and were leaking fuel every day, but it was cheaper to pay for the lost gas or diesel than the $40,000 for a new double-walled tank. The knowledge that fuels were being leaked into the groundwater all over the country was what prompted the federal mandate in the first place.

Most of our customers were coming from a religious organization that I will not name. They were being warned by their prophets that Y2K would be the end of the world, so get your food put away now. Well needless to say, when the year 2000 arrived it marked the end of our root cellar business. That's okay, we made some good money, and if the end of the world should come, Donnie and I know where a lot of food is stored.

In 1990 our oldest daughter graduated from high school, and then the next year our youngest daughter graduated as well. They both ended up going to work for a company called Heartland Nannies. This company sought out girls from rural communities in smaller towns, because they were more dependable and better workers than kids from the big cities. Also, they had very good safety protocols in case things didn't work out for whatever reason. If, say, the man of the house acted in any way inappropriate, one phone call to Heartland Nannies, and no questions asked, they would come to the girl's rescue and move her to a safe house. The girl could stay in the safe house until another family was arranged for, or they would fly them home. We felt very safe sending our girls off that way. Two years later in 1993, both girls married local boys, so the bird house was getting a little roomier. Say, you don't suppose they bailed out on me so quick just because I made them pick up cow chips?

Work on the twenty acres continued. I added two green houses and the aforementioned root cellar, a chicken house, and a summer kitchen for canning food out of the garden. We grew hay in the springtime, and rented pasture out to cow/calf pairs after the hay was removed. I built an ornamental pond out in front of the house, and Millie set to work planting flowers everywhere, so the place was really starting to look up.

It didn't dawn on us right away, but we came to realize we were turning another page of life. With both of our girls out of the house just like that, we got to thinking about the farm and all the food it produced. We decided that we had to sell Moo. She had a wonderful personality, and produced a lot of good-quality milk that we could no longer use, so we said good bye to our beloved brown-eyed bovine. We decided to sell the farm, but first we had to create a real house. I removed the first lean-to that had the bathroom in it, and replaced it with a two-story addition. It had three bedrooms, two bathrooms, a laundry room, and an entryway. That old farmhouse had a simple sort of charm that I've never been able to reproduce. We never paid insurance because we couldn't afford any. We didn't pay very much in taxes because we didn't have anything, and we never paid any interest because nobody would loan us any money. Life was simple back in those days, those "Good Old Days."

THE FOLLOWING ARE THINGS I LIKE:

The smell of lodgepole burning on a clear winter morning
When the air is so cold it's almost brittle, and the stars seem frozen in in their brilliance
To be the first one to make tracks in new fallen snow
The crisp silhouette of the mountains when the sun is setting behind them
Something old that works better than something new
The mortal lonesomeness of a meadowlark's song
A baby calf on its first romp
A child's admiration
A Good Wife
A good friend
A good dog
Young hands grasping old whiskers

"We All Got A Row To Hoe"

Words so truthful they feel good on your ears
The smell of warm, fertile earth, of coffee, of leather, of babies
Green beans just popping up in the garden
Making the final payment on a long loan
Spiders that stay outside
Mutual admiration
Breakfast, lunch, and dinner
The wisdom to sing praises when depressed
Someone who speaks only good of others
A swift blow when deserved
A friend who doesn't number your mistakes
Self-esteem
My best lifelong friend, my guitar
America

CHAPTER 18
FATHER AND SON'S GREAT ADVENTURE

The year was 1996 when we sold the farm, Millie's mom passed away, and my son Daniel and I did our great bike ride. The coming fall would be Daniels senior year, and I wanted to do something special with him, something we could both look back on. My girls had slipped out of the house almost unnoticed, so I didn't want that to happen again. I had an idea about what I wanted to do, but I kept it to myself. I knew once I mentioned it to Daniel, it would be set in concrete. I wanted to try things out a little bit with the new bicycle, a P38 Lightning I had just bought, to see if I thought I could even do what I was going to suggest we do. What I had in mind was a 600-mile bike ride from Montana to Sandy Oregon where my sister lived. I started riding out further and further on my bike until I could do thirty or forty miles no problem.

I knew Daniel would not have any problem with the ride. He had been crazy about bicycles from a very young age. Here in Montana, he had bought two bikes with his own money. Most kids his age would be looking forward to their first car, and for what he paid for his Specialized Stump Jumper, he could have bought a fairly good used car. When other kids his age we're out burning up gasoline and paying for high-priced auto insurance, Daniel was putting miles on his Stump Jumper. So, when I told him about the ride I was thinking about, he was all in 100%.

The first thing we had to do was get our bicycles ready for that ride. Daniel changed out his knobby tires for road tires, and borrowed some panniers from somebody. My bike was already a road bike, a recumbent. It was like a lawn chair on wheels, I loved it. But the only place I had for panniers was on the rack over my rear tire, and it was going to require something special. I took some measurements and made a drawing of what I thought would work, and gave them to Millie. She found some very heavy nylon material that would be strong enough. She did a great job, and the panniers fit my bike just perfect; I still have them today. There was lots of room for the tent, sleeping bags, and our Therma Rest sleeping mats behind my seat, and it added no wind resistance to my bike. We put together the camping gear we would need, which included a solar shower which I purchased for the ride. That shower worked great. Just fill it up with water out of the creek, lay it on a rock in the sun, and in no time at all you had a hot shower waiting for you.

We had driven Highway 12 over Lolo Pass many times over the years, so we knew the road well. But going on the bicycle was a completely different experience. There are, as I see it, two different types of travelers. First, there are those who make the journey the adventure; they stop at all the roadside attractions, wide turnouts that offer a great view of the river, or roadside signs talking about the adventures of Lewis and Clark. When stopping for gas, they are the ones most likely to strike up conversations with the fellow pumping gas next to him, and ask about local attractions. Then when paying for gas, they'll pick up a postcard or two to send off to friends and family, to share their adventure. They seem to make it from point A to point B just fine.

I am not that kind of traveler. I'm all about getting from point A to point B in the shortest possible time. Oh, I would like to stop and look at the signs, but then that pokey RV I passed three miles back would get in front of me again, and I'd have to risk my neck all over again to get around him on this windy road. Don't even think about going to the bathroom or getting something to eat. That will only happen when the car needs gas; got to keep those wheels turning. When I finally do get to my destination, the first thing I do is look at my watch to check my time, *"Hey, I cut twenty-nine minutes off my last trip,"* all while the car is sitting in the driveway with steam hissing out of the radiator, and the transmission is hot enough to cook a pork chop on.

Riding bicycles over that same road was a completely different situation, because it had nothing to do with time. It forced you to be in the moment, and stopping at whatever attraction was an absolute necessity when you're riding a bike. Plus, you hear things and see things you would never notice in a car, like the mountain goat that was knocking rocks off the cliffs right over our heads, the sound of the Lochsa River, the bird songs, and the chirping coming from the rock chucks. Oh, let's not forget smells! In a car you might catch the whiff of a skunk that lasts just a moment, but on a bicycle, you can enjoy that dead skunk for a good ten minutes.

With our bikes fully loaded, we could average ten to fifteen miles per hour, and faster on the downhills. The first day we made eighty-two miles just past Lowell, Idaho. We stayed in the Little Goose Campground. The next day continuing on Highway 12, we ended up making it all the way to Clarkston, WA, mostly because we couldn't find a place to camp. We had the river on the right and mountains on the left. We did 100 miles that day. The Chief Timothy Campground was only a few miles outside of Clarkston, but we were so tired we just stayed in the Motel 6 for the night.

A few miles past Chief Timothy Campground, the highway left the river bottom and went up over the top of the bluffs. That was a straight uphill climb of, I think six miles in length, top speed probably three or four miles per hour. It took forever to get to the top. About forty miles east of Clarkston we came to the little town of Pomeroy. I was riding through town on the sidewalk when I came to a spot where a car was parked blocking the sidewalk. I turned to the left to go back out onto the road, and that's when my front wheel skidded out on some sand, and I took the mother of all crashes. I got a road rash on my right hip the size of a football. It was Sunday; Pomeroy was closed down completely. We finally found a bar that was open, and asked if we could get a little first aid, water mostly to clean up the wound. Washington State had a law against minors in taverns, so even though it was just Dan, myself and the bartender, he wouldn't let Dan help me with the first aid. I think he had to stand out on the sidewalk. Some people just can't think outside of the box.

It hurt like crazy, but there was nothing to do for it, so we just kept on peddling. About four miles West of Pomeroy, we saw on the map what looked to be a cut-off road that would save us maybe ten miles. We had to go over the top of an extremely steep hill, which at the top turned to gravel and then descended on an even steeper decent down to the bottom were there was a creek. The name according to the map was Tucannon. It drained out of the Umatilla National Forest. We decided to spend the night there next to the Creek. There was an old abandoned chapel, and the place seemed a little sad. This had been a gathering place at one time. People probably rode in horse-drawn buggies or old Model T's to this little church. But when Highway 12 was built some years ago, it left this whole community abandoned. Now there was nothing left, just two tired bikers, one with a bad case of road rash.

The next morning, I was in a glorious amount of pain. Our first aid kit did not contain any kind of salve or ointment. There was nothing to do for it, so we just started cranking ourselves up out of the creek bottom, looking forward to a day of fine and pleasant misery. We estimated according to the map that we had a good thirty miles of gravel road to get back to the pavement, not a fun piece of work with skinny little road tires. So much for shortcuts. We won't be doing that again.

We accomplished almost eighty miles that day, and stayed right next to Wallula, in a camp named Sand Station. It had been a long, hot day, and we must have looked like a couple sticks of beef jerky. Some ladies camping next to us started giving us all kinds of food. We must have packed on 6000 calories apiece that night, but it was okay because we were going to need it. The best was yet to come.

The next morning, we crossed the Columbia River at Umatilla, heading for Crow Butte Campground on the Washington side of the river. As I have stated earlier, we have driven this route in a car many times. All of our family members live in the Vancouver-Portland area, so we would go over at least once or twice a year for visits. There are two things that have a huge impact when you're on a bicycle that you don't even notice when you're in the car. First, the forty-mile-per-hour head wind that we were presently plowing into on our bicycles was just awful. Second, Highway 14 runs up over the bluffs, then down to the river, then back up over the bluffs, and down to the river. It does this over and over again the whole length of the river, whereas Highway 84 on the Oregon side is pretty much down on the river the whole way. Pulling up a long, steep hill in the face of that forty-mile-per-hour wind was almost more than we could bear. So many times, I would look down at my speedometer to see that I was only going four to five miles per hour. We started looking forward to eighteen-wheelers coming up behind us, because they would punch a hole through the wind and give us a slight reprieve.

When traveling cross-country the way we were doing, you would pick up what you would have for dinner and breakfast in the last town you passed before the campground. The town before Crow Butte was called Roosevelt. We pulled in there on our bikes, only to find that the town was without a store or restaurant of any kind. That night we cooked up what we were carrying for emergency rations, two packages of Top Ramen noodles. They had a snack shop at the campground where we were able to get a couple miniature boxes of cold cereal; that was breakfast. We could have a real breakfast when we got to the next town, which was only about twenty-five miles away. We were still on Montana time, so we got out of camp pretty early. I was hoping the wind would not be so ferocious in these cooler morning temperatures. But as soon as we turned west, the wind was back, and instead of taking two hours to get to the next town, it took four.

"So," I'm thinking, *"what could make this joyous event we were presently experiencing even better?"* Well for starters, this town didn't have a store or a restaurant either, and now it is thirty-five miles to Biggs Junction. I turned to my son and

said, *"Today, your youth, strength and vitality will be outdone by my single attribute. I know how to suffer."*

The wind was driving us nuts. It was a good ten miles per hour stronger than it had been back in Umatilla. If we got off our bikes and stood there, the wind was still pushing against us. Dan was thinking about crawling in a culvert just to get away from the wind for a little while. We had eaten any candy bars or peanuts that we still had, and we were getting pretty hungry. I started seeing the error of my ways. If we had started in Portland, we would've been blown all the way to Montana by now. We came to a freight train that was stopped in a siding, waiting on an approaching train. I told Dan if we could get our bikes thrown up on one of the flat cars, we could ride the train. I didn't care where it was going, because any place was better than this. It was about a quarter of a mile to where we could get down to the train, so we started peddling for all we were worth. The approaching train was starting to pass, so we knew we didn't have a long time to get there. The train in the siding had started pulling out and was picking up speed. By the time we got there, it was already moving ten or twelve miles an hour. I told Dan that I would probably get my bike thrown up on the flat car, and then not be able get myself up there. Then I'd be stuck out here in the middle of nowhere with nothing.

Peddling uphill into the wind, we finally came to the top of a bluff, and there sitting just as pretty as you please was that beautiful Mount Hood. We could finally see our destination. It gave us both a big boost. We had to drop down off the bluff to the railroad tracks again, but we knew there was only one more push, one more long hill. We could see the bridge that crossed over the Columbia River into Biggs Junction on the Oregon side, and there were lots of restaurants there!

But I had come to the end of my reserves. I was pushing as hard as I could, but when I looked down at my speedometer, I was only going three miles per hour, and that's all I could do. If I went any slower, I'd fall over. I had nothing left to give. It was then that Daniel came alongside, put his hand on the back of my seat, and started to push. I watched in disbelief as my speedometer climbed to seven, then eight miles per hour. He pushed me all the way to the top of that hill. I think Dan was ready for dinner.

We spent the night there in a motel, and at 8 o'clock in the morning we called Millie, who was just getting ready to leave Montana. We planned to meet up in Hood River, only forty miles away. The wind was as ferocious as ever, maybe even more so the closer we got to Hood River. To our amazement, Millie drove the 500 and some miles in the same amount of time that we went forty miles against the wind. We caught a ride with her up behind Mount Hood, from where we had initially thought we would ride down to my sister's house. But when we got up to the backside of Mount Hood, the wind was blowing hard as ever. We decided that we had acquired an entire lifetime supply of pedaling into the wind. We rode the pickup down to the end of my sister's driveway, where we made our victory ride the last half mile.

This is what we looked like after 550 miles!

CHAPTER 19
THE BITTERROOT RIVER

In 1998 I started building a house on a one-acre lot on the Bitterroot River. It was a wonderful location, and the only house I have built using professional house plans. It was a beautiful house, and is still the nicest house on river road. All told, in a twenty-year span I built four complete-build houses, one new construction unfinished, and did a rebuild on a mobile home on a one-acre lot.

When the house on the river was finished in 2000, we started going to Arizona for the winters. I bought a piece of property in a little town called Amado, just south of Green Valley. It was an unusual little lot, and nobody saw any value in it. I've always had the ability to visualize a project to its conclusion, and I saw potential. I created a very livable space for two RVs, with a great view of the Santa Rita Mountains to the east. I only paid $13,000 for the lot, and some years later when we left, I sold it for $45,000. We continued going south for the winter until the arrival of the "China Flu" in 2020.

The river house had a huge picture window in the living room that looked out on the Bitterroot River. I spent many hours sitting there or on the small deck off of our bedroom upstairs watching bald eagles, osprey, and blue herons fishing in the river. When the eagles or osprey dove after a fish, it was so loud you could hear them hit the water from inside the house. It sounded like somebody smacking a board flat on the water as hard as they could. It was my observation that the osprey could out-fish the eagles four to one. The land on the other side of the river was part of the Lee Metcalf Wildlife Refuge, so our view of the Bitterroot River was not much different from what Lewis and Clark saw when they came right by here in 1804. This view was the inspiration for a song I wrote entitled

LOOKING OUT MY WINDOW

When a bird sets a wing and glides in the air,
It seems such a graceful thing.
When they dance with the wind it's a joy to my heart,
And lightens the load of care.
And the God of birds is blessed by these, for they do as
he intends.

Trees grow tall with leaves so green,
And provide a home for the birds.
Cool and green and shady they grow
To comfort a weary soul.

And the God of trees is blessed by these, for they do as
he intends.

And the river that flows beyond the trees,
From the rain to the brook to the sea.
Then the water goes to the sky from the sea,
And greens the earth for me.
And the God of rain is blessed by these, for they do as
he intends.

God made man as his final act
To see what he would be.
Would he gladden the heart and comfort the soul?
Would he be like the birds in the trees?
And the God of man is blessed by those who do as
he intends.

In 1998 I started a ministry that turned out to be very successful. Our pastor stopped by our house one day with a box full of song books, the old gospel songs in large print. I took the box of books and my guitar down to the local care center, and asked if they thought a one-hour sing-along would be something that people would enjoy. Well, they were very excited about my offer, and we settled on Tuesday mornings at 10 o'clock. The first day there were twelve or fifteen people that showed up, and I wanted to get to know them right off the bat. I went around the room and introduced myself to each one there. I came to one lady who was unresponsive. I was told her name was Dorothy. I said "Hello Dorothy, my name is George and I've come here to sing some old gospel songs that I hope you will remember." She was only able to make a grunt to acknowledge my presence. After one hour of singing these old gospel songs, I went around the room again to say goodbye to each one. When I came to Dorothy, I said, "I hope you enjoyed this time of singing these old songs." To my surprise, Dorothy came back with "I liked it very much, and you be careful driving home." Wow! What a difference. She was so closed down when I saw her the first time, now she was alive, the lights were on, and she was smiling. That was a big encouragement to me, and I knew I was on the right track. Over the years that followed, we all saw this same thing happen over and over again. Music has such a power to lift the soul. We became as big as bingo, and that's saying a lot in a nursing home.

The first couple of Tuesdays I was by myself, then my wife joined me, and then a lady by the name of Nancy from church came and played the piano, along with my guitar. It just grew from there. I bet all told, more than thirty people got involved in that ministry that ran for twenty-three years, every Tuesday morning without fail. I need to give a special thanks to Connie, her three daughters Kila, Cadence, and Natalie, and their son Shane. Connie and her kids always had a special song that they had worked on, or a poem, or story. I could not have continued as long as I did without their help. As a matter of fact, we grew to love them so much that we decided to adopt them. That gave me four more grandchildren to add to the eleven I already had, not a bad move. When the "China Flu" hit, we were promptly kicked out, so we sang outside the windows in the heat of summer into the fall, until it got so cold my guitar wouldn't stay in tune. Over the long years that we ministered at the care center, there were many times that the 10 o'clock sing-along was the highlight of our week.

When the river house was finished, I found I had more time on my hands, so I involved myself in music. I wrote some good songs during that period of time. For example, I'd like to share with you a song entitled "Wisdom." It came to me in a little different way than usual. My youngest daughter, Jennifer, came by for a visit one day, and told me she had a dream of writing a song about wisdom. I told her I thought that was a good idea, and I encouraged her to write the song. For the next month, every time I saw Jennifer, I told her that I had been thinking about what she could write, and how to get started. I said "wisdom is an eternal attribute of God. You could talk about wisdom's involvement in creation, redemption, and the end times. God's wisdom is freely given to all who would ask for it." Jennifer was a busy mama, and she didn't think she had the gift to write a song. But I don't know if it's a gift or a discipline. Dyslexia played a big part in my inability to spell, and I was so self-conscious about it. I wouldn't even write something in a Christmas or birthday card in fear that I would misspell a word. Today I use talk-to-text on my computer, and it makes things a lot easier. But to my surprise, I discovered my computer misspells words all the time. At any rate, I did write the song, and I hope you enjoy these words.

WISDOM

Wisdom was in the dark swirling eddies that gathered together in planets and stars.
In the cold dark vacuum what wisdom had won was the glory to God when creation was done.
When the heavens were finished and life first begun, the stars made the music for the words wisdom sung.
And wisdom was there on the very last day, when God fashioned Adam from carbon and clay.
Wisdom was there before we were a thought in God's mind.

Well known to wisdom but a mystery to man, a place called Golgotha and God's precious lamb.
Redemption would come to Adams lost seed when God, our Redeemer, was nailed to a tree.
Angels were ready to pull Christ away, but the master's great plan would be finished that day.
Wisdom so perfect so far beyond man, only God in his love could conceive such a plan.
Wisdom was there before we were a thought in God's mind.

With fear of the Lord wisdom begins, for wisdom will show us the depth of our sin.
Come foolish, come simple, come broken today, and you'll have the wisdom that formed DNA.
When the trumpets have sounded the judgment of man, only mercy will be for heirs of the lamb.
A new heaven and earth forever will be a day of rejoicing for you and for me.
Wisdom was there before we were a thought in God's mind.

For ten years I led music for the fourth and fifth-grade boys out in the Montana wilderness at Camp Utmost. Every day ended out around the campfire; we would sing songs, hear testimonies and scripture readings. On the last night, I would sing a Marty Robbins song called, "The Masters Call." It was a big hit with the boys.

For a period of a year or more I had the opportunity to lead singing at the chapel in the Montana State Penitentiary. It was a 200-mile round trip, so I was only able to go a couple times a month. I was there for the Wednesday night Chapel service, and I really enjoyed it; what a great church! I liked it more than my own home church. There was no hypocrisy there; everyone wore the same orange jumpsuit, and you don't get one of those for skipping choir practice. They were all sinners, and they knew it. That's the place every one of must start with God, for we are all sinners before him. Here's a song I wrote for those men, and I hope they are still singing it.

GOD SEEKER

Today my life is this prison, far from a mother's love.
I think in my heart, "How did I ever start on a road that's brought me so far!"
I know that cold rolled steel and concrete did not build this prison I'm in.
The heart is God's throne, but mine was like stone, and that's where all prisons begin.
Chorus
So, I want to become a God seeker, faithful, chosen, set free.
I'm going to become a God seeker, find God's creation in me.
Repent and become a God seeker, a new heart, a new life you'll see.

Today there are so many prisons built in the heart of mankind.
Looking for peace in a world of deceit, they follow satan's design.
Believe in this lie, then in prison you'll die, far from the Father's love.
Chorus

CHAPTER 20
LIFE ON THE BIG DITCH

We bought land that lay adjacent to what the old timers called, "the big ditch." There are a lot of irrigation ditches in the Bitterroot Valley, but this was the "big one," and it watered almost all of the useable farmland on the east side of the Bitterroot Valley. It has been in operation for over 112 years, and its official name is the Bitterroot Irrigation Ditch, or BRID. We didn't have any water rights from the big ditch, but it didn't matter, because it leaked profusely across most of our property. Our five acres was heavily timbered, and that is what drew me to the property in the first place. We started building a two-story house with a daylight basement. We were just getting started on framing the house up, when the BRID decided to line our section of the ditch with a plastic tarp to stop the leaking. When they stopped the water, a good twenty of the largest ponderosa pines were killed for lack of water. I mean for 100 years they had been getting all the water they ever needed, and they weren't able to survive without it. I suppose I could have sued the BRID for the loss of my trees, but my wife said, "Oh, just let it go, it is what it is." You know, I just hate that statement "It is what it is," because it leaves absolutely no room for sniveling. Oh well, if life gives you lemons... Fred, a friend of mine who is a logger by trade, came and cut the trees down, and bucked them to length, so I could send them to a sawmill southwest of us and have them cut into lumber. We used that for making board and bat siding for the house. We built a garage out of it, and my son made cabinets for the kitchen, and doors for the house, plus we had a lot of firewood, so it wasn't a total loss.

My sons-in-law, Scott, owned and operated a timber frame company, and I asked him if he could design and build a timber frame roof support for the house I was building. My son, Daniel, was working for him doing the design work at the time. I asked him if he could make it a ridge beam support rather than trusses. It would cost less, and give the living room a really open cathedral ceiling look. As the stick frame part of the house was being built, and the timber frame rafters were getting made, I saw a really big pine tree with a double top that we had to cut out of the footprint of the house. It had just been lying there the whole time, and I thought maybe it would make a good support timber for the ridge beam. Long story short, we used that log. It ended up being thirty-three feet long. The butt end of the log sat on a big stone in the basement, and the top went all the way up to support the ridge beam. After the roof was finished on the house, I built two spiral staircases out of steel and wood that wrapped around that ridge support tree, one going from the basement to the main floor, and the other continuing on up to the loft. On the main floor, I built a stick frame wall three feet high around the circumference of the staircase, with an eight-foot diameter. At first, we just covered it with sheetrock, but as the house was coming to completion, I started looking at that round and thought it would look really cool to make it look like a big wooden wine barrel or vat. I would need to use recycled wood so it would look like old weathered wood. I would have to cut three-foot-tall slats of wood that would stand vertically all around the stair case, making it look like a big vat. Also, I had some copper pieces left over from making the countertops, that I could make into straps that would look like stays in a barrel. But where would I find the wood? Then I remembered an old bridge crossing the ditch that the BRID had torn out about a mile upstream from our house.

So, one day my wife and I, along with two of our grandsons, Liam and Reuben, walked up the ditch road to have a look. The whole bridge had been pushed up into a pile with a Caterpillar. On closer examination, I saw that the three-inch-thick decking used on the bridge was in pretty good condition. There were also some heavier pieces that must have been bridge support timbers that were also usable. So, we all started pulling the best pieces we could find out of the pile that would be burned later that year. We dragged them down to the ditch and made two bundles, that I tied together with some baling twine I found lying around. When we were ready, I rolled the first bundle into the water, and my two barefoot grandsons hopped on. I pulled the next bundle into the water and climbed on it. Millie declined an offer to ride along. She would walk along with us as we floated back to the house. The older of the two grandsons, Liam, said he felt like Tom Sawyer and Huck Finn floating their rafts down the Mississippi River. The only thing they lacked was corncob pipes. We all enjoyed the one-mile ride down the ditch to where I could pull them out and get them in the back of my pickup. More happy memories to put in my vault.

Spiral Staircase

I had intended to do some work outside one day, but as it turned out, rain shut that whole project down. So, I sat in the living room looking out at a solid wall of clouds where the mountains used to be, and I wrote down this poem. I hope you enjoy it.

ODE TO A RAINY DAY

Mountains we think impervious to all that troubles man,
Mountains like the great divide that separate our land.
We think them quite unfeeling, just the bony part of earth.
We blast, and dig, and tunnel through for gold, that's all they're worth.

The fiercest storms God can throw hit peaks that scratch the sky,
Unmoved, unfeeling so we think, because they never cry.
But mountains are misunderstood, today I saw it clear,
Mountains show a tender side to something they hold dear.

It's clouds that come and settle down, too heavy for the air,
Mountains hid in their embrace, enthralled in tender care.
Clouds of cotton gently touch and kiss the weathered face,

Unlike frost or blazing sun, these clouds bring healing grace.

Clouds give mountains what they want, what can never be,
Hid from ever gawking eyes, its anonymity.
From time to time, they need a rest, a place we're not allowed.
When tired of paparazzi, they summon fluffy clouds.
It's okay, I need a rest. Confine me to my chair.
Enjoy the respite from our eyes. Enjoy your love affair.

Millie and I were coming home from Missoula on a Sunday afternoon, when we got a phone call from one of our neighbors, who informed us that there was a gigantic forest fire heading right for our house. As we got closer to home, we could see the smoke from miles away. When we got home, we saw our house was just fine, and there were fire trucks everywhere. There were three trucks in our backyard, three more up on the ditch road pumping water down to the fire, and a couple more down below. It took two or three days to get the fire completely out, because it would keep flaring up here and there. I remember we woke up one morning and the place was all full of fire trucks again, because the fire had flared up in the night and one of our neighbors had called it in.

It turns out that the neighbor to the north of us started the fire. His girlfriend was there with her kids, and they wanted to make S'mores. There was a total ban on burning at that time, you couldn't even have a charcoal fire in your barbecue. So, I started proceedings against his homeowner's liability coverage, and it took forever, I mean a good year, to finally get them to settle up.

In the meanwhile, we had decided it was time to sell the house. We started looking for land, and here is where a really cool, let's call it a miracle, happened. We found a place that would be just right, the one we're on now, and it was only $34,500. That was a pretty good price, because any buildable lot at that time was going for $50.000. The only problem was, the pile of money we were living on from the sale of the last house was almost gone. So, we were living off of our "Social Insecurity," and there was nothing left over for land payments. We were still waiting on the insurance company to settle up on the fire damage done to our property. I didn't know what they would offer for payment of the trees lost in the fire, I thought maybe $15,000 or even $20,000. That would go a long way towards the purchase of the property. The insurance company was taking so long to settle up with us that I ended up calling the Montana Insurance Commissioner. They got back to us finally and offered, to my surprise, $29,000. I was delighted with that, but I didn't let on. Insurance companies tend to low ball you on the first time around. I thanked her for the offer, but said if I really wanted to replace the lost trees, it would probably cost more than that. She got back to me in a couple of hours and offered $34,000 for damages. Then I asked her something that surprised her and myself as well. I asked "How do you feel about that?" Well, she was not expecting a question like that! The phone went dead for a about half a minute, and she finely came back with "How about $34,500?" Cha Ching!!! Thank you, Lord! We got the next building property for free.

CHAPTER 21
BEAR CUB LANE

I built a thirty-by-forty-foot steel shop building and drilled the well on the new property. So, when the house on the five acres sold, we had a place to move our fifth wheel where it would have electricity and water. We had all of our belongings in the shop, and we had set up a corner with our couch, chairs, and TV set. I had two electric heaters running in the shop as well.

Building this house, Millie worked with me almost every day. On the last house she was still doing medical transcription. This time Millie ran the chop saw, and did a very good job of it, and I ran the nailer. Except for the concrete and the roofing, we did everything ourselves, the framing, plumbing, and electrical. We hung the sheetrock, did the taping, mudding and texturing, and of course, all of the painting. This is the first house for which I made all of the trim for the floor, the doors, and the windows. I used side-cut Larch from my son-in-law's sawmill. I milled it, planed it, ran it through an edger, and sanded each piece. Then I did all the staining and clear coat. Each window took seven different pieces, and the whole process took most of the winter. I know of few women who are willing to work as hard as Millie worked on the building of this house. It took five years to finish it completely, of course that's not factoring in spending winters in Arizona.

When our house on the big ditch sold in the fall of the year, we moved onto the property and lived in our twenty-four-foot fifth wheel. It was initially our intention to stay in Montana until after Christmas, but on December 17 the temperature dropped to twenty-five below zero. Now if you have ever owned an RV, you know that they were designed for summertime down at the lake. We had an electric heater running nonstop, and the propane furnace doing the same, and it still felt cold. If you reached inside one of the cabinets for something, it felt like reaching into a freezer, and our undies froze to the wall. There was a huge icicle the size of my leg running down the side of our fifth wheel, over a tire, and into a straw bale we had for insulation. Earlier in the fall, I had asked our friend Fred, the logger who had fallen our trees, how he kept the black water tank from freezing. He and his wife were self-employed loggers, who often worked late into the fall, living in their trailer out where there is no electricity. Fred told me that was no problem, you just use RV antifreeze to flush with. A word to the wise: RV antifreeze will not freeze up hard like water, but at twenty-five below zero it turns into something like very firm Jell-O. I will spare you the details.

As we huddled in our fifth wheel trying to keep warm, Millie decided to do some Christmas cards. She handed one to me and asked if I would write a note in a card to our sister-in-law, Sharon. So, I worked on it for a while, and here is what I wrote to her;

Dreadful cold and frozen toes, and snow all piled around.
The wind blows down from the angry sky, till we're frozen far from town.
Insulation, not so much, and heaters all but fail.
We're going to pick some pockets, 'cuz it's, warm down in the jail.

Merry Christmas.

Sharon told me later that she laughed her head off for over a month after she had gotten that card. Our electric bill for that December came to $447.00! For the next two years we only stayed in Montana until Thanksgiving.

When we got back in the spring from Arizona, we parked our trailer next to the shop and hooked up to the power and water. The Stevensville Irrigation Company had turned the water on, so the ditch that ran along our west property line was running full of water. A neighbor lady and her granddaughter would come down to visit, because the little toddler just loved our dog, Rudy. Almost every day they would show up at some time whether we were busy or not. Sometimes, she would seem oblivious to the fact that we were trying to build a house, and we had nothing better to do than visit with her.

Anyhow, one day she and her husband were there for a visit, and their granddaughter was playing with Rudy. They had been there for about five minutes, long enough for the little girl to collect a big pile of pine cones for Rudy. Then I heard the grandmother say "Where did she go?" What happened next was from the Lord, for when I heard her say that, a thought went through my mind like an arrow through a strawbale, just three words; "worst case scenario." Without any hesitation I looked sharply to my right at the irrigation ditch. I saw nothing, so I moved over to the corner of our fifth wheel so I could see further down the ditch. There she was, floating face down in that dirty water!!! I thought if I was ever going to have a heart attack, it would have been right in that moment. I started to run to get to her as quickly as I could, but there was a bunch of scrap lumber thrown in a pile like jack straws. There was no time to go around; I had to go right over the top, praying all the while that I wouldn't stumble and fall. I jumped in the ditch, and as I landed, I was falling to my left, but I was able to reach over with my right hand and snatch her out of the water. She coughed right away, so I knew she had been holding her breath. CPR would not be necessary.

This whole episode didn't take more than eight or nine seconds and it was over, with a happy ending! Her grandfather made it down to where we were, and I handed her off to him. The water had been cold, and I told Millie she had to take them all home in the pickup, and get the little girl into dry clothes. I went in to take a shower. My adrenaline level must have been running at 110%, and I was shaking, not from the cold but from the thought of what could have happened. After I got cleaned up, I took a handful of pine cones and walk down to where I knew she would have gone. There was kind of a natural path leading down to the water. I threw the pine cones into the water and followed them down the ditch, counting off the seconds until I got to where I pulled her out; fourteen seconds. If we had spent even a few seconds looking on the other side of the car, under the pickup, or around the corner of the shop, she would have been out of sight. How long, I thought, would it have taken to come to the horrific conclusion that she must be floating down the ditch somewhere?

Within a month I had built a five-and-a-half-foot stock fence all around the property, so that could never happen again. Millie and I have often thought if that little girl had been lost that day, we could not have stayed on that property. We would have had to sell it and move on.

CHAPTER 22
So Many Blessings

Back in 1979 I had written a wedding song for a couple that we knew from bible school, and we have used that song so many times. I remember singing it at my sister's wedding, and then at our kids' weddings, and now at our grandkids' weddings.

The Wedding Song

Time often gauges our promises made.
It will show you the value of the vows you've just made.
And time gives the answer to so many questions,
Time gives us children, wisdom so fine.

So, in time you'll watch your precious love grow,
It started with romance, but with age you will know
Real love just never happens, it's something that grows.

Everything living has needs to survive,
Your love is no different, without care it could die.

You must love one another as Christ has loved us,
His love was thoughtful, gentle and kind.

There was more to it than this, but it kind of gives you an idea, and how true it has turned out for Millie and I. Our eleven grandchildren have now produced eleven greats so far. I'm trying to keep up with all the new names to remember. But knowing their ages is more than I can handle. I hear this one is fourteen months, and this one six months, and the next one is twelve months. So, I thought I would try and figure out how many months old I am, and it turns out that on my next birthday I'll be 900 months old. Wow! Thanksgiving this year will be at grandma and grandpa's house; I think the guest list will number thirty-nine.

One last thought from the dreamer:

So today I will a dreamer be, don't leave the busy
work to me.
My troubled soul today must gain a respite from this
nagging pain.
A dreamer like a worldly monk, from sun to sun upon
his bunk,
He thinks the thoughts deep in his soul, pursuing
dreams his only goal.
It's no waste but a life well spent, caring not for
food or rent.

So Many Blessings

Tomorrow a builder I may be, but today these words are enough for me.

Thanks for coming with me through all these years.

Back in the vault, the little boy that is me never gets old. The memories get old but I, we, were created as immortal beings from the beginning. This is evidenced by the fact that people from every corner of the globe all have some kind of understanding of a deity. It doesn't mean everybody's right, but it shows that it's in our DNA. There is indeed "Evidence That Demands a Verdict" (Josh McDowell and Sean McDowell).

I'm looking around the inside of the vault at the piles of paper, the boxes full of memories and the shelves that line the wall, all the things we have been looking at. The only thing left is what's under the tarp, the bad things covered up in the middle of the floor. I wonder, the vault is the safest of places, so why the tarp? No one can see in here. Is it to protect me from what lies beneath the tarp, from what I have done? I suppose. What are the things that I'm so very ashamed of? Is it not the same for all of us, the lust of the flesh, the lust of the eyes, and the pride of life? Worse than that, according to Matthew chapter 5, I am an adulterer and a murderer.

There are two things, if we still have a functioning conscience; number one, we are all ashamed of what's under the tarp, at least we should be. Number two and more importantly, God is holy, and we are not. We're sinners, more than that, we are sinners by nature and we try to hide the fact, from others, from God, and obviously from ourselves. We're going to need a bigger tarp! I can make a pretty good guess about the things that are under your tarp, so this becomes a universal problem. All mankind are debtors deserving death and spiritual separation from God. So, is there a universal solution for our condition? As a matter of fact, there is; "For God so loved the world that he gave his only son, that whoever believes in him shall not perish but have eternal life." (John 3:16). What does this look like? "If you confess with your mouth that Jesus is Lord and believe in your heart that God raised Him from the dead, you will be saved. For with the heart, one believes and is justified, and with the mouth one confesses and is saved." (Romans 10:9,10). What about all that stuff under the tarp? "As far as the east is from the west, so far does He remove our transgressions from us." (Psalms 103:12).

I walked over to the center of the vault, right in front of the tarp. I reached down and picked it up by a corner; but there was nothing there! What I held in my small hand was not a tarp at all. It was a robe; it had become a white robe. A word came to me from one of the prophets of old: "I will greatly rejoice in the Lord; my soul shall exult in my God; for he has clothed me with garments of salvation. He has wrapped me in the robe of righteousness."

I put on the robe, and the whole vault was filled with a glorious light. "In him was life, and the life was the light of men. And the light shines in the darkness…"

For the King of Righteousness sits on His throne
In a city, it's not far away,
And the saints of the ages are singing His praise
I must be a part of that song
We'll all be a part of that song
A song of creation, a song of His love,
It's the praise song of eternity.

CPSIA information can be obtained
at www.ICGtesting.com
Printed in the USA
BVHW091949030223
657824BV00016B/1507

9 781662 867217